THE ARROW

AVRO CF-105 MK.1
PILOT'S OPERATING INSTRUCTIONS
AND RCAF TESTING/BASING PLANS

Foreword by
Lieutenant Colonel T.F.J. Leversedge

FOREWORD

1999 represents both the 75th anniversary of the Royal Canadian Air Force (RCAF) and the 40th anniversary of the demise of the Avro Arrow aircraft. The Avro Arrow is an important part of Canadian heritage. It has become not only a significant symbol in Canadian history but also part of Canadian myth and legend — what might have been? There has been much written about the Arrow and its story, some of it fact and some pure fiction. These pilot operating instructions and the original plans from the RCAF are, however, part of the real history of a significant aircraft. The instructions clearly document the sophistication and the level of performance of the initial prototype aircraft and give an intriguing glimpse into the follow-up plans for the aircraft. Indeed, the prototype aircraft exceeded all of the performance data contained in this manual, and had the project continued, it would have needed significant amendment. Similarly, the RCAF's plans for the scheduled introduction of the aircraft were comprehensive and precise. They give some idea of the scope of the program and the level of effort involved in introducing a new aircraft into service.

The original Avro Arrow Pilot Operating Instructions (classified Secret) were issued to company test pilots and to test pilots of the Royal Canadian Air Force, who were assigned to the test program. Fortunately, several library copies survived including a copy sent to the RCAF's Central Experimental Proving Establishment, which has now become the Aerospace Engineering Test Establishment, in the Canadian Forces.

This replica book that you now hold in your hands faithfully reproduces the information contained in these now unclassified manuals. While every effort has been taken to duplicate the exact content of the document (including some mistakes and inconsistencies), some minor changes have been made to the format to allow for the differences of modern computer fonts compared to their typewriter counterparts. Additionally, the once secret RCAF documentation on the Arrow aircraft that was part of the National Defence plans of the period has been replicated (again complete with some spelling mistakes and inconsistencies) to show the original contents. However, a significant change in the original document format, from horizontal 8" x 14" to vertical 8.5" x 11", has been made to facilitate publishing this document along with the pilot's instructions.

For those intimate with the Arrow program's changes and difficulties, the RCAF's documentation shows how the program was running into schedule difficulties, with the impact of delays and the eventual cancellation of the ASTRA weapons systems. Finally, some material and a glossary of terms have been added in a completely new centre section to complement the pilot instructions and explain the context of the RCAF material.

In this anniversary year, it is fitting that this information is now unclassified and available to the public. The sophistication of the aircraft and the professionalism of those involved should be clearly apparent to all concerned.

Special thanks to R. Kyle Schmidt, John Bradley, Ron Page, Don Pearsons in 1 Canadian Divison Headquarters, and the Canadian Forces Directorate of History and Heritage, along with the Directorate of Intellectual Property, for assistance provided in the preparation of this reproduction.

Lieutenant Colonel T. F. J. Leversedge
July 1999

MASTER TABLE OF CONTENTS

Table of contents for revised format.

PRELIMINARY PILOT'S OPERATING INSTRUCTIONS - ARROW 1

PRELIMINARY
PILOT'S OPERATING INSTRUCTIONS
ARROW I

APRIL 1958

(This issue supersedes issue dated January 1958 due to
the addition of Parts 1, 2 and 3 and revision to Part 4.)

AVRO AIRCRAFT LIMITED

MALTON - ONTARIO

TABLE OF CONTENTS

Original.

PRELIMINARY PILOT'S
OPERATING INSTRUCTIONS — ARROW I

PART I
DESCRIPTION

INTRODUCTION

General

1.   The ARROW I is a delta wing aircraft powered with two Pratt and Whitney J75 - P3 engines with afterburners.

Airframe

2.   The fuselage, wings, vertical stabilizer and control surfaces are of all metal construction. The tandem bogey main wheels and legs are attached to the inner wing main torque box and retract inboard and forwards. The nose wheel is located beneath the pressurized cockpits and retracts forwards. The flying control surfaces are fully powered by two independent hydraulic systems. Speed brakes are fitted below the fuselage and a brake parachute is installed in the aft end of the fuselage. Space in the radar nose and armament bay is utilized for test equipment and instrumentation.

Engines

3.   The J75-P3 engine is a continuous axial flow turbojet. Two tandem compressors, one low pressure and the other high pressure, with their respective turbines form two rotor systems which are mechanically independent but related as to airflow. A hydro-mechanical fuel control establishes the power output. The engine is provided with a low pressure compressor speed limiter which reduces fuel flow when a predetermined low pressure compressor rpm is exceeded. The engine has an installed military thrust on a standard day at sea level of approximately 12,500 lb.

4.   The engine incorporates an afterburner, the operation of which is automatic after it has been selected by the pilot. The afterburner increases the available engine thrust by approximately 50%, giving a installed maximum thrust on a standard day at sea level of approximately 18,500 lb.

5.   An anti-icing system prevents icing on the inlet section of the engine and a de-icing system is employed on the duct intakes.

Dimensions

6.   The dimensions of the aircraft are as follows:

  (a)   Length - 73 ft 4 in. (To datum)
             Length - 80 ft 10 in. (Including probe)

  (b)   Wing Span - 50 ft 0 in.

  (c)   Height - 21 ft 3 in. (To top of vertical stabilizer - unloaded aircraft)
             Height - 14 ft 6 in. (To top of canopy)

(d)   Sweepback - 61° 27' (Leading edge)
        11° 12' (Trailing edge)

(e)   Wheel Track - 30 ft 2-1/2 in.

FUEL SYSTEM

General

7.   Fuel is carried in two bladder type tanks in the fuselage and six integral tanks in each wing. The forward fuselage tank and the six wing tanks in the right wing normally feed the RH engine, while the aft fuselage tank and the six wing tanks in the left wing normally feed the LH engine. The only interconnection between each sub-system is the crossfeed. One of the wing tanks in each sub-system functions as a collector tank. Each sub-system supplies fuel to its respective engines by means of a collector tank booster pump driven by a shaft from that engine. Each booster pump has sufficient capacity to supply the maximum fuel demand of its own engine and afterburner, or to supply the demand of both engines with partial afterburning. The fuel passes from the booster pump to an oil-to-fuel heat exchanger and a low pressure fuel cock before entering the engine compartment.

8.   A long range fuel tank of 500 gals capacity may be fitted (in later aircraft) on the under side of the fuselage for ferry missions. Fuel from this tank feeds into the collector tanks.

(See Figure 1-1 FUEL SYSTEM FEEDS (Aircraft) in colour section p 18).

Fuel Tank Capacities

9.   The fuel capacities are give imperial gallons and are for usable fuel. Weights are for JP4 fuel, specific gravity .78.

	Gal.	Lb.
Tank No. 1	263	2051
Tank No. 2	259	2020
Tank No. 3 (151 gal - 1162.5 lb)	302	2355
Tank No. 4 (90 gal - 693 lb)	180	1404
Tank No. 5 (146 gal - 1124 lb)	92	2278
Tank No. 6 (154 gal - 1186 lb)	308	2402
Tank No. 7 (279 gal - 2148.5 lb)	558	4352
Tank No. 8 (173 gal - 1332 lb)	346	2699
TOTAL:	2508 gal	19561 lb
Long Range Tank	500 gal	3900 lb

Arrow #204 taxiing during part of the flight test programme.

On a cold winter morning, Arrow #203 is ready for flight.

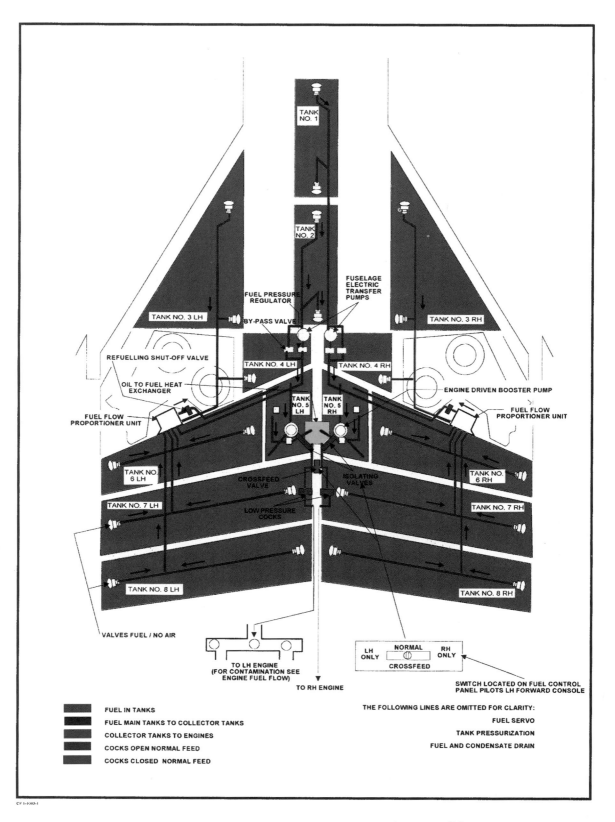

FIG 1-1 FUEL SYSTEM FEEDS (Aircraft)

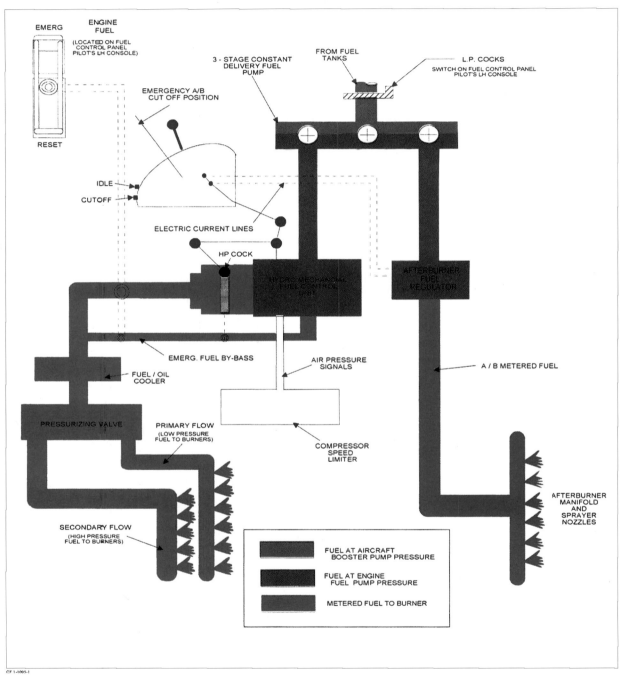

FIG 1-2 FUEL FLOW (Engine)

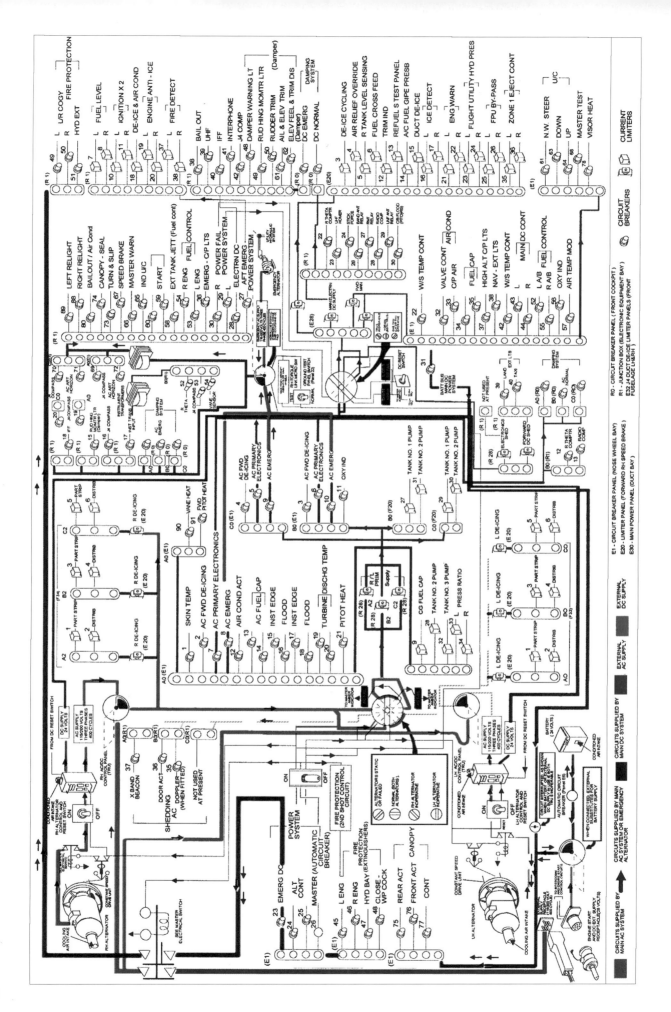

20

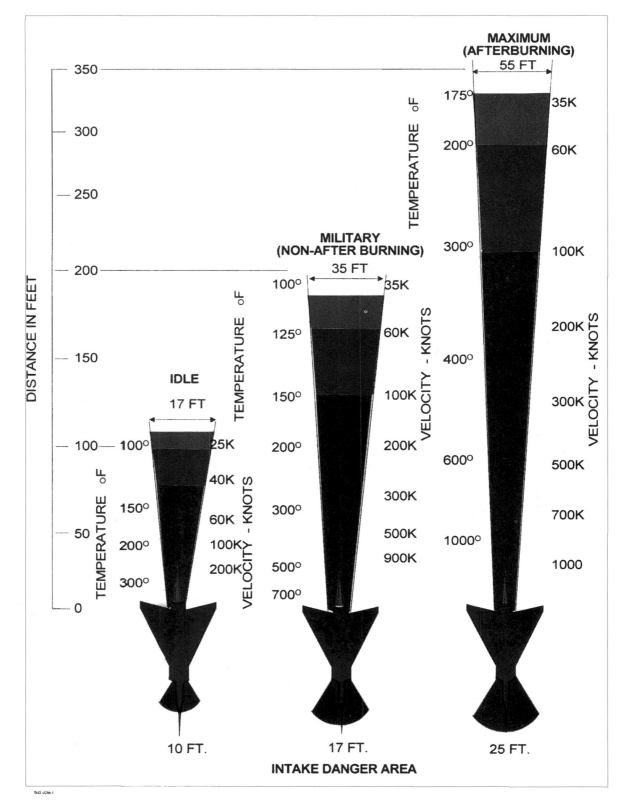

FIG 2-2 JET WAKE AND INTAKE DANGER AREAS

AT LEFT: FIG 1-3 ELECTRICAL POWER SUPPLY SYSTEM

A fully developed drag chute was used in the test programme landings.

Fuel Flow to the Engines

10.   Fuel is supplied from the fuselage tanks and wing tanks to the respective sub-system fuel flow proportioner (para 11) by tank pressurization. An electric transfer pump at each fuselage tank outlet increases the delivery pressure from these tanks to equalize the difference in pressurization between the fuselage tank and wing tanks, so that fuel from all the tanks flows into the proportioner at 19 psia (25 psia in the first aircraft).

11.   The fuel flow proportioner meters fuel from the tributary tanks to ensure that all tanks empty in the same elapsed time. Fuel flows from the proportioner by a single pipe into the sub-system collector tank. The collector tank is normally maintained full, except during negative 'g' conditions or during a sustained high rate of roll. Delivery from the collector tank is maintained under these conditions by having inlets at the fore and aft corners of the tank.

12.   Normally, fuel is delivered from its sub-system collector tank by a booster pump, shaft driven from the engine accessories gearbox of the engine on that side. From the collector tank the fuel passes through a heat exchanger. Downstream of the heat exchanger the two sub-systems are interconnected by a crossfeed valve. The crossfeed valve is controlled by a switch in the pilot's cockpit, and remains closed under normal conditions. A low pressure cock is fitted between the heat exchanger and each engine.

(See Figure 1-2 FUEL FLOW (Engine) diagram in colour section page 19).

Fuel Tank Pressurization

13.   All fuel tanks are pressurized by engine bleed air taken from the air conditioning system downstream of the ram air heat exchanger. The purpose of this is to achieve fuel transfer and also to prevent fuel boiling.

14.   Pressure in all wing tanks is regulated to 19 psi absolute. (25 psia in the first aircraft.) Pressure in the fuselage tanks is regulated to a 10 psi differential. Transfer from each fuselage tank, due to the difference in pressure between these tanks and the wing tanks, is assisted by an electrically driven transfer pump.

15.   To prevent over-pressurization through failure of air regulator, an air pressure relief valve is fitted in the air system to the wing tanks. This valve is also used as a means of venting pressure from the tanks during ground pressure refuelling. A similar valve is fitted for the fuselage tanks and performs the same functions as the wing tank valve and, in addition, it prevents over-pressurization during rapid climbs by releasing air to limit the differential between tank pressure and atmospheric pressure.

Fuel System Controls

16.   A high pressure cock is fitted for each engine at the engine side of engine fuel pumps and is operated during the aft portion of travel of the throttle levers. Moving the throttles up and back from the idle position closes the HP cocks and terminates the fuel supply to the engines.

17.   The low pressure cocks are controlled by two switches on the fuel control panel, marked LP FUEL COCKS and are protected by guards.

18.   A three-position CROSSFEED switch is fitted on the LH console immediately aft of the throttles and is marked LH ONLY-NORMAL-RH ONLY. In the NORMAL position the crossfeed valve is closed and the isolating valves are both open. During single engine flying, in order to maintain the weight of fuel on either side approximately equal, the switch is selected to the inoperative engine side alternately with the NORMAL selection, to balance the fuel. On the second and subsequent aircraft when crossfeeding from the inoperative engine side, the FUEL PRESS warning light of the operating engine will illuminate, as the booster pump on the failed side is not operating. When selected to LH ONLY, the crossfeed valve is opened and the RH isolating valve is closed. The LH isolating valve remains open; thus fuel is supplied from the aft fuselage tank and LH wing tanks only. To supply fuel from the front fuselage tank and RH wing tanks, the crossfeed switch is selected to RH ONLY. This opens the crossfeed valve, closes the LH isolating valve and opens the RH isolating valve. On the NORMAL selection, with the inoperative engine throttle lever at cut-off, the operative engine will obtain its fuel supply from its own side sub-system.

Engine Fuel System Emergencies

19. Two ENGINE FUEL toggle switches, protected by guards, are located on the fuel control panel on the LH console to allow selection of emergency fuel should failure of the flow control unit occur. The switches are of the three-position type, with EMERG and RESET positions marked. The switches are spring-loaded from RESET to the centre or normal fuel position. When guards are closed the switches are automatically set in the normal fuel position. In this position the engines are automatically controlled by speed, temperature and pressure sensing devices to obtain and hold the thrust selected by the pilot.

20.   When a guard is raised and the switch is selected to EMERG, the automatic fuel flow control unit is by-passed and fuel flow, partially compensated for altitude, is then directly controlled by power lever movement. The ENG EMERG FUEL warning light will illuminate when the emergency fuel selector valve is fully open.

CAUTION

When operating in the EMERG fuel selection, the turbine discharge temperature must be closely monitored. Power must be reduced immediately if there is any tendency for the temperature to increase beyond limits. Rapid throttle movements must be avoided as the emergency system does not provide the automatic overspeed, overtemperature, flame-out or compressor stall prevention features of the normal fuel control system.

21.   As the compressor inlet pressure decreases with altitude, fuel flow to the engine also decreases. The emergency system will provide at least 95% military thrust on a 100° F day at low altitudes and at least 80% of military thrust at altitudes up to 30,000 feet.

22.   The engine may be started on the emergency system, either in flight or on the ground. The afterburner may be operated on the emergency system, in which case the throttles must be operated carefully to prevent engine overspeed and over-temperature.

23.   During training or testing, and with a properly functioning fuel control system, the transfer back from EMERG to the normal system may be made. The throttle control for the affected engine should be retarded to the idle position, and the appropriate engine fuel toggle switch moved and held in RESET for five seconds. This selection will open the selector valve to the normal position and the ENG EMERG FUEL warning light will go out. The switch, when released, will take up the centre position and the guard should then be closed.

CAUTION

The solenoid operated fuel selector valve will not be energized if the switch is only moved back to the normal or centre position. The solenoid is energized in the RESET position, and then de-energized when the switch is allowed to return to the centre position.

Long Range Fuel Tank Supply

24.   To be issued later.

Fuel Warning Lights

25.   Warning lights for the fuel system are located on the warning panel fitted to the forward RH console. The master red and amber warning lights are located on the main panel.

26.   Individual amber warning lights for the fuel system are marked and indicate as follows:

(a)   FUEL LOW - Two lights are fitted to indicate low level of fuel in the LH or RH collector tanks. The illumination of a FUEL LOW light should always be accompanied by the illumination of the FUEL PROP light as the low level switch also operates the flow proportioner by-pass. Provided the FUEL LOW light illuminated through failure of the fuel flow proportioner, the automatic opening of the proportioner by-pass will allow fuel to flow to the collector tank and the FUEL LOW light will then go out. If the light stays on it indicates approximately 740 lb of usable fuel is remaining on that side.

(b)   FUEL PROP - One light is fitted and indicates one of four conditions, or a combination of these conditions, as follows:

(1)   A fuel flow proportioner has failed and the by-pass has opened. The relevant FUEL LOW warning light will also illuminate and remain illuminated until that side collector tank fuel level exceeds the low level limit. It will inform the pilot that automatic control of the fuel centre of gravity has ceased and violent manoeuvres or sustained operation at high altitude must be avoided.

(2)   Failure of the LH or RH fuselage electric transfer pumps to deliver a differential pressure in excess of 3 psi, due either a pump failure, lack of fuel in a fuselage tank,or loss of prime of a fuselage pump. The pump by-pass will automatically open and allow fuel from the fuselage tank to flow to the proportioner, but at a decreased pressure. At high altitudes fuel from the fuselage tank will not be used in proportion to fuel from the other tanks.

(3)   Either the RH or LH refuelling access door (one in each main landing gear well) is open. On the second and subsequent aircraft the door will not close if the gate is closed, which is the position used only for refuelling. This ensures that a take-off is not carried out with the gate valve in the closed position. In this position, fuel is prevented from entering the collector tank from the fuel proportioner. Only collector tank fuel would be available on that side with the gate valve closed.

CAUTION

On the first aircraft it is possible for the door to be closed with gate valve in the closed position. The FUEL PROP light only indicates the door open condition. Therefore, on the first aircraft, the exterior inspection prior to flight must include a check of the gate valve position. The two positions are marked FLIGHT POSITION-VALVE OPEN, and VALVE CLOSED-REFUEL AND DEFUEL. The flight position of the gate valve on the RH side of the aircraft is 'up' while this position on the LH side is 'down'.

(4)   The refuelling master switch on the master refuelling panel located adjacent to the LH speed brake is ON. (The access door of this panel will not close if the switch is ON.)

(c)   ENG EMERG FUEL - One light is fitted which illuminates when either the LH or RH toggle switch marked ENGINE FUEL on the LH console is selected to EMERG. The light is extinguished when the toggle switch is held at RESET for five seconds and then allowed to return to the centre position.

(d)   ENG FUEL PRESS - A light is fitted for each engine and illuminates when the fuel pressure at the engine inlet falls below 18 psi, and indicates failure of a booster pump. The pump by-pass will automatically open and allow fuel to be delivered by a combination of tank pressurization, engine pump suction and gravity, at rates adequate to supply that engine at military power. If fuel tank pressurization fails when operating above military rating, the light will also illuminate.

Fuel Tank Contents Indicators

27.   Two indicators marked FUEL QUANTITY LBS x 1000 are fitted on the pilot's main instrument panel. The left hand indicator registers the weight of fuel in the left hand tank sub-system, while the right hand indicator registers the weight of fuel in the right hand tank sub-system. The indicators register continuously while the master electrical switch is ON.

OIL SYSTEM

General

28.   The oil system on each engine is entirely self-contained and automatic. An oil tank with a usable capacity of 2.9 Imp. gals. (3.5 U.S. gals) is fitted on each engine.

Oil Pressure Warning

29.   Warning of a drop of oil pressure to below 25 psi is given by the illumination of the master amber warning light and an amber light for each engine oil system on the warning, marked OIL PRESS.

ELECTRICAL SYSTEM

General

30.   The aircraft is equipped with two 30 KVA 120/208 volt, ram air cooled alternators. One alternator is fitted to and is driven by each engine through a constant speed unit for AC power supply. In addition to supplying the aircraft AC services, each alternator supplies a transformer rectifier unit. The TRUs operate in parallel and provide 27.5 volts DC for the DC services. A hydraulically driven emergency alternator is fitted and supplies essential AC services in case of complete electrical failure. The aircraft battery supplies essential DC service for a limited period during this emergency.

See Figure 1-3 ELECTRICAL POWER SUPPLY SYSTEM in colour section (page 20)

Master Electrical Switch

31.   The master electrical switch is located on the forward RH console below the warning panel and is marked MASTER ELEC ON-OFF. The switch controls the complete electrics of the aircraft with exception of the services taken from the battery bus which are as follows:

(a)   Engine and hydraulic bay fire extinguishers.

(b)   Canopy actuation.

(c)   Emergency alternator solenoid.

(d)   LP cock operation to closed position only. (OFF).

Warning and Indicating Lights

32.   The warning and indicating light system in the pilot's cockpit consists of the following:

(a)   One red and one amber master warning indicator, located at the top centre of the main instrument panel. The indicators are fitted with double filament bulbs.

(b)   A warning panel on the RH forward console, consisting of 25 amber lights, a master warning light PRESS-TO-RESET switch, a PUSH-TO-TEST switch and a DAY/NIGHT dimmer toggle switch.

(c)   Two red ENG BLEED warning lights located on the RH console immediately below the warning panel.

(d)   Three red fire warning lights located on the LH console immediately behind the throttle levers, marked FIRE - LH/HYD/RH.

(e)   A warning light fitted in the landing gear selector lever. (See Hydraulics - Landing Gear).

(f)   A green NAV BAIL OUT indicating light on the top centre of the main instrument panel.

33.   The warning light system in the navigator's cockpit consists of a red BAIL OUT warning light located on the main panel, directly in front of the navigator.

NOTE

When the red BAIL OUT light is illuminated, an audio oscillator is energized, giving audible warning for bail out in addition to the visual warning.

Master Warning Lights and System Warning Lights

34.   The master warning lights are used in conjunction with the individual system warning lights and provide a master indication any fault. They may be turned off by operating a PRESS-TO-RESET switch on the warning light panel. The system warning light will remain on, however, until the fault has been cleared. The PRESS-TO-TEST switch on the warning light panel is used to test the filaments of the following lights:

(a)   Master Warning Lights.

(b)   System warning lights on the panel.

(c)   Fire indication warning lights.

(d)   Air conditioning engine bleed warning lights.

(e)   Warning light in the landing gear selector lever.

(f)   NAV BAIL OUT light in the pilot's cockpit.

35.   The warning light panel has 25 lights covered by amber coloured lens caps, upon which is inscribed the system served. The lights function as follows:

(a)   FUEL LOW, LH and RH - indicates a low level of fuel in the LH or RH fuel collector tank. The FUEL PROP light will illuminate also.

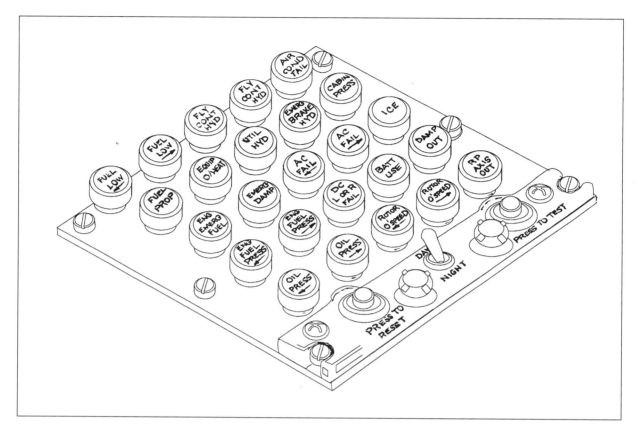

FIG-1-4 MASTER WARNING PANEL

(b)   FUEL PROP - Indicates any of the following four conditions:

(1)   A fuel flow proportioner has failed.

(2)   A LH or RH fuselage electric transfer pump has failed.

(3)   The LH and/or RH refuelling adaptor door(s) are open.

(4)   The master refuelling switch is ON.

(c)   ENG EMERG FUEL - Illuminates when the ENG FUEL switch is selected to EMERG.

(d)   ENG FUEL PRESS, LH and RH - Indicates that fuel delivery pressure to the LH or RH engine pumps is less than 17.3 psia. The light will go out if the pressure rises to 18.3 psia.

(e)   OIL PRESS, LH and RH - Indicates that the oil pressure of the LH or RH engine is 25 psia or less.

(f)   FLY CONT HYD - Two indicator lights are provided. The LH one serves the 'B' flying control hydraulic system and the RH one serves the 'A' flying control hydraulic system. They illuminate if the particular system pressure is less than 1000 psi.

(g)   UTIL HYD - Indicates when the utility hydraulic system pressure is less than 1000 psi.

(h)   EMERG BRAKE HYD - Indicates when the emergency brake accumulator pressure is less than 1600 psi, and is insufficient for the use of brakes upon landing.

(j)   AC FAIL, LH and RH - Indicates a phase failure in the LH or RH AC system, and will be accompanied by the illumination of the single light marked DC FAIL, L or R.

(k)   DC L or R FAIL - One light indicates for both T.R.Us. It will denote failure of both T.R.Us if the BATT USE light also illuminates. If the DC FAIL light illuminates on its own it will indicates that one TRU has failed.

(m)   BATT USE - Indicates when the aircraft battery alone is supplying the DC power.

(n)   ROTOR O'SPEED, LH and RH - Indicates when the LH or RH engine low pressure compressor is overspeeding.

(p)   CABIN PRESS - Indicates when the cabin altitude exceeds 31,000 feet.

(q)   AIR COND FAIL - Indicates when the air conditioning cooling turbine outlet temperature has exceeded 80°F. (On the first flights of the first aircraft the light will indicate a cockpit inlet temperature of more than 240°F).

(r)   EQUIP O'HEAT - Indicates when the equipment air supply temperature has exceeded 100°F.

(s)   ICE - Indicates icing conditions in either or both engine air intakes.

(t)   EMERG DAMP - Indicates that emergency damping on the rudder is in use. The R - P AXIS OUT light will also illuminate.

(u)   DAMP OUT - Indicates no damping system is operating.

(v)   R - P AXIS OUT - Indicates that the Roll and/or Pitch axis damping system is not operating.

Master Warning Control Unit

36.   The master warning control unit is located in the LH side of the nose wheel well and operates the warning lights in the following manner:

(a)   On receipt of a fire signal, the master RED warning will illuminate together the appropriate RED fire warning light.

(b)   On receipt of a signal from either the 'A' or 'B' flying control hydraulic system, the master AMBER warning light will illuminate together with the associated AMBER light on the warning panel. Should both 'A' and 'B' systems fail simultaneously or consecutively, both RED and AMBER master warning lights will illuminate together with both A and B system AMBER lights on the warning panel.

(c)   When the pilot selects Engine Emergency Fuel, the illumination of the appropriate AMBER light on the warning panel will remind the pilot that he is using this selection. No master warning light signal is given. In addition, the light will provide an indication to the pilot prior to take-off that an engine fuel system is energized to the emergency selection, coincident with an ENGINE FUEL selector switch being in the normal position. This would indicate that an engine had been shut down while operating on the emergency system, and that the selector switch had inadvertently been moved to the normal position without first being held in RESET for five seconds. The particular engine must be operating in order to make a selection of the ENGINE FUEL normal-emergency system.

(d)   Any of the remaining lights on the warning panel will be energized simultaneously with the master AMBER warning light on receipt of a warning signal.

NOTE

No master warning indication is given when the air conditioning ENG BLEED warning light or lights illuminate.

AC System

37.   The engine driven alternators supplying AC power are controlled by two switches on the RH forward console, marked ALTERNATORS ON - RESET - OFF.

38.   Failure of an alternator is indicated by the illumination the master amber warning light and the appropriate LH or RH AC FAIL light on the warning panel. This will also cause the DC FAIL light to illuminate. The alternator may be reset by moving the ALTERNATOR switch to RESET and back to ON. If the reset is successful the AC FAIL, DC FAIL and master amber lights will go out; alternatively, only the AC FAIL light may go out. In the latter case, the DC RESET button should be pressed, and a successful reset will be indicated by the DC FAIL and master amber light going out. If the fault has not cleared the AC FAIL will again illuminate, in which case the switch should be left in the off position.

39.   Normally, the RH alternator supplies the AC power requirements. Should the RH alternator fail, the LH alternator assumes the load. Should the LH alternator fail, no change in power supply will be apparent. The operating alternator will supply, through its TRU, all DC services except the landing and taxi lights.

40.   An emergency alternator is fitted to provide electrical power to essential services in the event of complete electrical failure by energizing a solenoid shut-off valve which diverts utility hydraulic fluid to a hydraulic motor which in turn drives the alternator. Sufficient power is supplied to operated the emergency damping system, artificial horizon, J4 compass and IFF until a relight is obtained. In case of a double engine flame out, one wind-milling engine will maintain sufficient utility hydraulic pressure to drive the motor.

DC System

41.   The transformer rectifier units (TRU's) are fed from their respective main AC bus-bars, and the output is fed to the main DC bus.

42.   Failure of a single transformer rectifier unit is indicated by the illumination of the master amber warning light and the DC L or R FAIL light on the warning panel. The operating TRU will provide all DC services except the landing and taxi light. Failure of both TRU's will be indicated by the illumination of the DC FAIL light and the BATT USE light on the warning panel. The illumination of the BATT USE light signifies that the DC supply to the emergency bus and battery bus is being taken from the aircraft battery. The main DC bus supply will be automatically shed.

43.   A push button switch is fitted on the RH console in the front cockpit marked DC RESET. If the DC L or R FAIL warning light illuminates alone or in conjunction with the BATT USE warning light, either or both TRU's may be reset, provided the fault has been cleared, by pressing the DC RESET button.

44.   The DC system maintains the battery charged, therefore if the BATT USE light illuminates, the battery is discharging. The following services will be available from the battery through the DC Emergency Flight Bus for approximately 20 minutes, depending on the original battery charge and the number of services operated:

(a)   Landing Gear Indication
(b)   Fire Detection
(c)   Canopy Seal
(d)   Speed Brake Actuation
(e)   Warning Light System
(f)   Emergency Cockpit Lights (Emer. Flood Light)
(g)   Turn and Slip Indicator
(h)   Ignition (Relight)
(j)   ARC/34 UHF
(k)   AIC/10 Intercommunication
(m)   DC Damping (Yaw)
(n)   IFF (APX/6A)
(p)   Hinge Moment Limiter
(q)   Engine Emergency Fuel Selection
(r)   Bail Out Indication

NOTE

The landing gear selector valve is operated by the main DC supply. If the BATT USE light is illuminated, the landing gear cannot be unlocked by the normal selection. However, it can be unlocked by using the emergency extension procedure. (See Part 3, Para 7.)

Engine Starting Services

45.   The engines may be started individually or simultaneously by motoring of a ground starter cart which supplies compressed air to the turbine starters and a 28 volt DC supply for ignition. Leads from the cart to the aircraft comprise two air hoses and an electrical supply connector. Incorporated in the connector are intercommunication leads which allow the pilot to communicate with the ground control centre, the navigator, and the ground starting crew. These connections are automatically withdrawn from the aircraft by means of lanyard releases when the aircraft commences to taxi. When the aircraft is being towed, a lead from the towing vehicle to the aircraft receptacle enables intercommunication between the cockpit occupant and the driver of the towing vehicle.

46.   When the supply connector from the ground starter cart is plugged into the aircraft receptacle, the aircraft battery supply is automatically cut-off, thus preventing any drain on the aircraft battery during starting. (Not applicable to the first aircraft.)

47.   The starting system consists essentially of an air turbine starter and an ignition system for each engine. The air supply to the air turbine starters is controlled by the ENGINE - START/OFF/RESET switches, one for each engine, which are spring loaded to OFF. The ignition supply is energized by a centrifugal switch operated when an engine speed of 700 rpm is attained. A second centrifugal switch is operated at 3020 rpm, to de-energize the ignition system.

48.   An ENGINE START switch may be momentarily selected to RESET if it becomes necessary to interrupt the starting cycle. This de-energizes the 'locked' starting relay and resets the system for a further start. The RESET position is also used for motoring the engine without ignition.

49.   An external supply socket is also provided for an external supply of AC current. This supply should be plugged into the aircraft prior to engine starting to enable AC instruments, particularly the turbine discharge temperature gauge, to operate. The supply is also used for ground servicing checks. On later aircraft, an AC supply from the starter cart will be available.

FLYING CONTROL SYSTEM

General

50.   The ailerons, elevators and rudder are fully power operated, utilizing hydraulic pressure supplied by two pumps on each engine. The hydraulic components are controlled electrically or mechanically through cables and linkages; there being no direct mechanical control.

51.   There are three modes of control of the aircraft in its final configuration, the normal mode, the automatic mode and the emergency mode. The automatic flight mode will not be installed in early aircraft.

52.   In the normal mode, a damping system automatically stabilizes the aircraft in all three axes and co-ordinates rudder movement with movement of the ailerons and elevators. Control in the normal mode is by means of an electrical force transducer fitted in the control column handgrip.

53.   In the automatic flight mode (when fitted), the damping system is operative as in the normal mode, but aileron and elevator position is controlled by an Automatic Flight Control Sub-system (AFCS). The AFCS allows the aircraft to be controlled from the ground for Automatic Ground Control Interception (AGGI) or for Automatic Ground Control Approach (AGCA). It also provides certain pilot assist functions by holding any set course or altitude, or it may hold any set Mach number by varying the aircrafts pitch attitude. It also provides for automatic navigation by controlling the aircraft according to information fed into a dead reckoning computer by the navigator. An AFCS disconnect push button switch is fitted on the control column handgrip. When the AFCS is disconnected by this switch, the damping system reverts to the normal mode.

54.   In the emergency mode the hydraulic components for operating the ailerons and elevators are controlled mechanically. Yaw stabilization and rudder co-ordination are maintained by an emergency yaw damping system.

55.   Pilot feel at the control column is provided by the damping system in the normal mode, and by spring feel in the emergency mode.

56.   If certain flight limitations are exceeded, the system automatically changes over to the emergency mode.

57.   Elevator and aileron trim is obtained by means of a four-way switch on the control column, while rudder trim is obtained by a toggle switch on the pilot's LH console. Trimming alters the position of the entire control surface. A CONTROL SURFACE RESPONSE indicator is mounted on the LH console and shows the amount of movement of the control surfaces in relationship to the main surface. In the case of the rudder and elevator, movement of these control surfaces will be shown in the natural sense on the indicators. In the case of the aileron, movement of the ailerons will be indicated as the resultant wing movement from the trim action; i.e. LW DOWN and RW DOWN. In later aircraft to reduce elevator trim drag at altitude, the ailerons are automatically deflected upwards by means of a pressure switch, which operates at approximately 45,000 feet. The switch opens when the aircraft descends to 42,000 feet and the ailerons return to their normal position.

Hydraulic System

58.   Two independent hydraulic systems are employed, one pump on each engine supplies the 'A'; system while the other pump on each engine supplies the 'B' system. The supply is 4000 psi; an accumulator in each system prevents fluctuations. The lowering or loss of pressure in a system to 1000 psi or less will illuminate the appropriate warning light on the warning panel. The lights are marked FLY CONT HYD and the LH light indicates for the 'B' system, while the RH light indicates for the 'A' system.

59.   The 'B' system supplies the control surface actuators and damping servos for pitch, roll and yaw damping. The 'A' system supplies the control surface actuators and damping servo for emergency yaw damping.

60.   In the event of loss of one engine or loss of one system, adequate control is still available. Rates of control movement may be slower with one engine failed. With either system failed, the available 'g' at high speeds will be restricted. With the 'B' system failed the aircraft will be in the emergency mode of flying control.

Ram Air Driven Turbine (Not fitted on the first flights of the first aircraft.)

61.   In later aircraft a ram air driven turbine is installed in the LH side of the fuselage for use in the event of a two-engine flame-out. When selected by the pilot, the turbine extends horizontally into the airstream thus driving a hydraulic pump. The pump is connected to the 'A' hydraulic flying control system and supplies sufficient hydraulic pressure to enable the flying controls to be operated at all speeds from 350 knots down to a landing speed of 140 knots.

CAUTION

The maximum speed for extending the ram air turbine is 350 knots EAS.
The aircraft must not be flown above this speed with the turbine extended.

62.   The turbine is extended into the airstream by a jack operated from the utility hydraulic system, and controlled by a switch on the RH console marked RAM AIR TURBINE.

NOTE

Under a two-engine flame out condition, the utility hydraulic system maintains its pressure from the windmilling engines. Should one engine be seized, the single windmilling engine will maintain the pressure.

63.   Under a two-engine flame out condition, emergency AC power is maintained by the emergency alternator driven by a motor through the utility hydraulic system, provided that at least one engine is windmilling.

Damping System

64.   The damping system provides artificial stabilization in flight. Unstable tendencies are picked up by sensors and adjustments are made to the control surfaces. The pilot is unaware of the corrections being made. As the damping in the yaw axis is of major importance in the higher speed range, duplicated electrical and hydraulic supplies are installed for the rudder control. The damping system comprises three distinct channels, the pitch channel which controls the elevators, the roll channel which controls the ailerons and the yaw channel which controls the rudder.

65.   Switches for controlling the damping system are located on the pilot's LH console, and on the control column. Eight DAMPING CIRCUIT BREAKERS are fitted outboard of the DAMPER control panel. The rear group of four are in the NORMAL damping circuit, while the forward group of four are in the EMERGENCY damping circuit. The breakers are a protection against excessive current drain and will not reset if the circuit is overloaded. They also provide a secondary means of switching should the normal means of damper disengagement fail to operate. Mounted on the DAMPER panel are the following controls:

(a)   A POWER ON-OFF toggle switch protected by a guard. When selected "ON" power is supplied to the damping system and AFCS.

(b)   An ENGAGE push button switch for engaging the normal mode of operation, or for re-engaging the aileron or elevator damping if they have been automatically disconnected through excessive manoeuvring. Normal mode must be selected before the emergency mode can be selected.

(c)   An EMERG push button switch for selecting the emergency mode of damping (i.e. to disengage the normal mode). This switch will be deleted on later aircraft.

66.   Two push button switches are fitted on the control column grip. One switch reverts the damping system to the emergency mode (i.e. it disengages the normal mode) acting the same as the EMERG switch on the DAMPER panel. The other switch disengages the AFCS system (if fitted), and leaves the damping system in the normal mode.

67.   In the normal and AFCS modes, damping is effective on the elevators, ailerons and rudder. When the landing gear is selected down damping of all the control surfaces is modified as follows:

   (a)   In the roll axis, sufficient damping is retained in order to help in counteracting "dutch roll", (in conjunction with the yaw axis).

   (b)   In the yaw axis, the modified damping allows intentional sideslip to be introduced, although any transient yaw will be corrected.

   (c)   In the pitch axis, damping is retained to a limited extent. Any excessive instability left uncorrected by the damper will be easily counteracted by the pilot.

   (d)   Pilot "feel" at the controls changes. (See para 77.)

68.   In the emergency mode only rudder damping is effective.

NOTE

In order to test the damping system when the aircraft is on the ground and simulate landing gear UP conditions, a DAMPER TEST push button marked U/C UP MODE is fitted at the rear of the LH console in the pilot's cockpit. Depressing and holding the button will disengage the landing gear "down" micro-switch and allow damping system to be checked as in a landing gear "up" condition.

Damping System Warning Lights

69.   Malfunction of the damping system is indicated by the illumination of the master amber warning light and the system warning light or lights on the warning panel. Three lights are fitted on the warning panel for the damping system. They are marked and function as follows:

(a)   EMERG DAMP - Illuminates when emergency damping only is in operation, i.e. damping is operative on the rudder only, and can occur for the following reasons:

      (1)   By automatic reversion to the emergency mode by excessive sideslip or side acceleration.(See para 90). The R/P AXIS OUT light will also illuminate.

      (2)   By manually selecting EMERG on the DAMPING SYSTEM panel or the disengage switch on the control column. The R/P AXIS OUT light will also illuminate.

(b)   R/P-AXIS OUT - Illuminates when either the elevator and/or aileron damper is cut out automatically by excessive pitch or roll. (Provisionally 4-1/2 to 5 g in pitch and 159° per second in roll.) It will also illuminate in conjunction with the EMERG DAMP light.

NOTE

After the manoeuvre the axis or axes may be re-engaged by pressing the ENGAGE switch on the damper panel.

(c)   DAMP-OUT - Illuminates when all damping is inoperative and can occur for the following reasons:

      (1)   When the master electrics switch is turned on after entering the aircraft and the DAMPER POWER switch is either OFF, or ON with no mode selected.

      (2)   When a change over is made to emergency mode for any reason but the 'A' hydraulic system, supplying the emergency yaw damper, is unserviceable.

NOTE

An emergency alternator automatically supplies AC power to the emergency damping system (also to the artificial horizon, J4 Compass and IFF) in case of complete electrical failure.

PITCH AXIS

Pilot Command Control

70.   In the normal mode of flying control, when the pilot exerts a force on the control column grip to move the elevators, a force transducer on the control column transmits an electrical signal. Similar signals are transmitted by ground control, when the AFCS mode, without pilot operation of the control column. In both cases the signals are fed to servos, which convert the electrical signals into a mechanical movement by means of hydraulic pressure. The servos are known as parallel (or command) servo and differential (or damping) servo. Additional signals enter the differential servo, depending upon outside forces acting on the aircraft, to maintain stability. These servo units alter the position of the elevator control valves through linkages and quadrants. The valve movement directs the hydraulic pressure to the appropriate side of a hydraulic jack, resulting in movement of the elevators.

71.   In the normal mode, the electrical output at the transducer is directly proportional to the force exerted at the grip. The control column will move as the force is exerted, as with a conventional flying control system, but it is not moved directly by the pilot. Movement of the control column follows the positioning of the elevators by the command circuits, but as the response of the system is instantaneous, the control column will appear to be moved by the pilot.

72.   In the normal and AFCS modes the hydraulic pressure in the parallel servo can be overpowered by a force of 70-90 lb. at the control column (the force depending upon flight conditions) although the imme-diate action for a malfunction in these modes would normally require dis-engagement of the particular flying control system in use at that time.

73.   In the emergency mode the parallel servo is disengaged. Movement of the control column does not send electrical signals from the transducer to the parallel servo, but moves cables and a mechanical link system which operates the hydraulic actuator control valve. Thus the elevators are finally moved by hydraulic pressure as before.

Trim Control

74.   In the normal and emergency modes, up and down movement of the trim button will result in movement of the elevator control surfaces. In the normal mode the control surface movement is achieved by the transmission of an electrical signal which moves the elevators in the same manner as would hand pressure on the control column.

75.   In the emergency mode, a feel-and-trim unit is called into use. This unit is a spring-loaded assembly which supplies a feel on the control column during flight in the emergency mode. When the aircraft is trimmed, an electrically operator actuator changes the neutral length of the feel-and-trim unit, to move the elevators up or down as required. The unit also ensures that upon a change-over from the normal mode to the emergency mode there is no movement of the elevators and pilot feel remains unchanged. However, a change in feel will be noticeable upon moving the control column after the change-over. A 'g' bob-weight is fitted at the end of a lever in the elevator control system. The purpose of the weight is to induce a load on the control column under 'g' conditions, and so make the control column progressively more difficult to pull as 'g' is increased. When no 'g' is being imposed a balance spring counteracts this weight. In the normal mode of control the bob-weight is not felt at the control column due to the normal feel system.

76.   The emergency mode trim unit is not called into use during the normal mode of control but rides freely, although any seizure of the unit or a runaway trim motor would, unless guarded against, affect movement of the elevators. A switch operated release mechanism is fitted. The switch, protected by a guard, is located on the pilot's forward LH console and is marked ELEV TRIM-DISENGAGE.

Pilot Feel in the Normal Mode

77.   An electrical feel system is used for normal mode flight. The stick force required to move the elevators is made to feel proportional to the amount of 'g' pulled. For a particular 'g' the stick force requirement is constant irrespective of speed or altitude. With the landing gear selected

down, feel is directly proportional to the degree of displacement of the elevator control surfaces, without regard to airspeed or altitude. (Pilot feel in the emergency mode - See para 75.)

G Limits

78.   The stick force transducer is set to limit pilot imposed 'g' to a value of 4-1/2 to 5 g, but if through component malfunctions this value is exceeded, the normal mode of control in the pitch axis disengages automatically and control reverts to emergency mode. Upon change-over the aircraft may require to be manually re-trimmed. In the emergency mode, the 'g' bob-weight is felt at the control column under 'g' conditions. G limiting is then under the control of the pilot.

79.   The pitch axis will also disengage should the yaw axis monitor operate due to excessive skid, sideslip or transverse acceleration. (See para 90.)

ROLL AXIS

Pilot Command Control

80.   In all modes of flying control the operation of the ailerons by means of signals, or by cables, is identical to the operation of the elevators. (See para 70.) Components in the system differ slightly - for instance in place of an accelerometer, the aileron system utilizes a roll rate gyro, but from the pilot's point of view, the systems operate in a similar manner.

81.   In the medium speed range, the system is designed to produce a rate of roll in proportion to the force applied to the control column handgrip. At high or low speeds the force required for a given rate of roll is increased slightly.

82.   When a turn is initiated and the required amount of bank angle is obtained, release of pressure at the control column grip will return the ailerons and the control column to the neutral setting. The turn will be maintained by elevator; "holding off bank" will be required but to a lesser extent than on conventional aircraft. Damping on the roll axis is in effect at all times.

83.   When the landing gear is selected down, movement of the ailerons is directly proportional to control column movement. With the landing gear up airspeed is a governing factor in amount of aileron movement, within the limitation set by the maximum roll rate of 159° per second.

Turn Co-ordination

84.   When force is applied to the control column to initiate a turn, signals are transmitted which effect the deflection of the rudder in a direction appropriate to turn the aircraft and over-come adverse yawing movement resulting from the aileron movement. When the aileron ceases its movement, the rudder is automatically returned to its neutral position. Any further yawing moment in the turn is counteracted through a transverse accelerometer affecting the yaw damper.

Trim Control

85.   In the normal mode of control, lateral trim is obtained by operating the control column trim button in the appropriate direction until the ailerons have moved the desired amount. In the emergency mode of control the effect of moving the trim button is the same, although aileron movement is obtained by means of the trim actuator instead of through the command servo. Electronic feel of the ailerons is cut out during the emergency mode of control. The springs of the feel-and-trim unit have to be compressed when the control column is moved, thus providing feel. A pressure trim circuit ensures smooth re-engagement upon change-over from emergency mode to normal mode; however, the aircraft may require to be trimmed laterally for straight and level flight in the normal mode.

Roll Rate Limits

86.   To prevent overstressing the aircraft structure, the roll axis damping system disengages if the roll rate exceeds 159° per second. The system will also disengage should the yaw axis monitor operate due to excessive skid, sideslip or transverse acceleration. (See para 90.)

YAW AXIS

General

87.   The yaw damping system provides directional damping and rudder turn co-ordination when in the normal mode of control. The system is duplicated in order to provide emergency yaw damping and turn co-ordination in the event of failure of the normal system, or should control of the aircraft be reverted to the emergency mode. Should failure of the electrical supply to the damping system occur, an emergency hydraulically driven alternator automatically supplies power for emergency yaw damping.

88.   In all modes of control, rudder is automatically co-ordinated with aileron movement. In an emergency in the normal mode, the rudder may be moved by means of the rudder bar if sufficient force is used. A force-switch is incorporated which requires a force of thirty pounds to overcome.

89.   When the landing gear is selected down, the yaw damping signal is modified in order that a certain amount of intentional yaw may be applied by the pilot without opposition from the system. Although the pilot has this control if required, stability about the yaw axis is maintained.

Yaw Rate Limits

90.   Automatic disengagement occurs if, due to a fault in the normal damper system, 10° of sideslip is exceeded or the aircraft exceeds a preset yaw acceleration. Control of all three axes is then in the emergency mode,i.e. only the emergency yaw damping is effective.

Rudder Trim, Feel and Hinge Moment Limitation

91.   The rudder may be trimmed by a toggle switch located on the pilot's LH console marked RUDDER TRIM LEFT/RIGHT. Operating the trim switch moves an actuator, and through linkage alters the rudder hydraulic jack control valve. The movement of the rudder by the trim circuit changes the no-load position of the rudder bar.

92.   Rudder 'feel' is provided by a feel unit and the system also incorporates a hinge moment limitation linkage. The system functions automatically, and its action is to decrease the amount of rudder move-ment for a given force on the rudder bar as the aerodynamic loading on the rudder increases. This limitation also is effective in the trim circuit.

AUTOMATIC FLIGHT CONTROL SYSTEM (When fitted)

93.   In the AFCS mode, either pilot assist functions or fully automatic functions may be selected on the selector panel.

94.   The pilot assist functions are normal AFCS, mach hold and altitude hold. The automatic functions are Automatic Ground Control Intercept (AGCI), Attack, Automatic Navigation and Automatic Ground Control Approach (AGCA).

95.   In the normal AFCS mode heading hold, roll attitude and pitch attitude hold are maintained, provided certain attitude limits are not exceeded. Heading will be maintained provided the aircraft is not banked at an angle in excess of 7-1/2°. A change in heading is made by movement of the control column. This action will disconnect the heading reference when the bank angle exceeds 7-1/2°. The aircraft is then levelled at the new heading and the control column is released. This new heading will be maintained. If the control column is released during a turn, the turn will be maintained provided the bank angle is less than 76°. If the bank is more than 76° only stabilization in roll is provided. In the pitch axis, an angle of climb or dive will be maintained upon release of the control column, provided the climb or dive angle is less than 55°.

96.   Any malfunction occurring in the AFCS mode will call for immediate manual disengagement of the system, although in later aircraft this disengagement may be made automatic. In this case a warning that the AFCS had been automatically disengaged will be incorporated.

97.   A failure of the system when the aircraft is performing a 'g' manoeuvre will, by means of the spring of the trim unit, automatically ensure that 'g' is reduced in the patch axis to $\pm$ 1/2'g' of 1 'g' flight, provided no force is applied to the control column.

AIR CONDITIONING SYSTEM

General

98.   The air conditioning system is supplied with hot air bled from both engine compressors. A certain proportion of this hot air is cooled by means of three components; an air to air heat exchanger which cools engine bleed air by ram airstream, an air to water heat exchanger which cools conditioned air by heat transfer to distilled water, and a cooling turbine and fan. Various

types of controllers and air valves served by thermostats and sensors are fitted which serve to maintain the selected conditions of air in the system during various airspeed and altitude conditions.

NOTE

The temperature and pressure of the engine bleed air varies according to flight conditions.

99.   Ground equipment can be connected to the system for cooling the electronic equipment when the aircraft is on the ground.

100.   The air conditioning system fulfills the following functions:

(a)   Supplies hot and cold air to maintain cockpit pressure and temperature within the required limits.

(b)   Maintains the required temperature levels in areas where heat is generated by electrical and electronic equipment.

(c)   Supplies air for fuel tank pressurization, windscreen rain repellent (if fitted), the low pressure pneumatic system and the liquid oxygen converter. Discharged air from the cockpits is used to cool and scavenge the armament bay.

Cabin Pressurization

101.   The cabin pressure remains the same as the outside air up to 10,000 feet. Above this altitude the differential between cabin pressure and aircraft pressure altitude increases linearly until a differential pressure of 4.5-5 psi would be reached at 60,000 feet. A safety valve is fitted in the rear cockpit which opens to release cabin pressure if at any time it reaches 5.25 psi, and closes when pressure returns to 4.5 psi.

102.   Cabin pressure altitude is shown on a gauge fitted on the RH side of the instrument panel in the pilot's cockpit and is marked CABIN PRESSURE.

103.   A CABIN PRESSURE amber warning light is fitted on the warning panel. The master amber warning and the CABIN PRESSURE warning will illuminate if at any time the cabin altitude reaches 31,000 feet ($\pm$ 1800 feet) or higher.

Cockpit Controls

104.   The air conditioning controls are grouped together on a panel at the rear of the RH console in the pilot's cockpit and comprise the following:

(a)   A temperature setting rheostat switch marked TEMP/COOL-WARM. Movement of the switch from COOL to WARM will result in an increase of cabin temperature within the range of approximately 40°F-80°F.

(b)   A DEFOG switch with ON/OFF positions. In the case of fog forming in the cabin, selecting the switch to ON will rapidly raise the cabin temperature to approximately 90°F thus

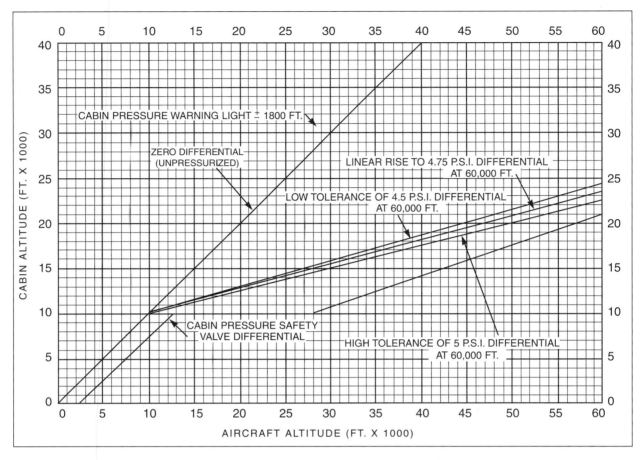

FIG-1-5 PRESSURIZATION GRAPH

overriding the rheostat temperature selection. An automatic control prevents the cabin temperature from rising above 140°F in case of failure of a temperature control component.

(c)   An AIR SUPPLY switch with NORM-OFF-EMERG positions which controls as follows:

(1)   In the NORM position air is delivered to the cabin at a temperature determined by the setting of the TEMP/COOL-WARM rheostat. Outlets in the cockpits are located on either side of the seats and at floor level. During taxiing and take-off the amount of air supplied to the cockpits is reduced. When the landing gear is raised after take-off a micro-switch is actuated which fully opens the cockpit air shut-off valve and allows full air supply to the cabin. Lowering the landing gear will reduce the air supply by nearly closing the valve. Pressurization of the cockpits commences when the aircraft reaches an altitude of 10,000 feet. During flight, the equipment areas comprising the nose radar, alternator control, oxygen converter, fuselage electronics, fire control, dorsal electronics and the aircraft battery are maintained at a temperature of between 80°–90°F by air from the system. The armament bay is cooled by discharged air from the cockpits, and this air also scavenges the armament bay of fumes.

(2)   In the OFF position, all valves in the system are closed; this selection is made under the following conditions, provided low engine rpm are not in use at the time.

a.   Upon illumination of the master amber warning light and the EQUIP O'HEAT light on the warning panel.

b.   Upon illumination of the master amber warning light and the AIR COND FAIL light on the warning panel.

c.   Upon failure of the cooling air flow to the cabin. At high speeds this will result in high cockpit temperatures due to kinetic heating.

To lower the temperature under the above conditions, (provided that low engine rpm are not the cause), the OFF position must be selected and the aircraft speed reduced immediately to below Mach 1.2. This selection will close the main air shut-off valve, and the cockpit air inlet valve, thus shutting off all air supply to the cockpit. A signal will also be supplied to shut off the electronic equipment in the nose radar compartment. (When radar is fitted). When speed has been reduced the switch should then be selected to EMERG, which opens the ram air supply valves.

(3)   In the EMERG position emergency ram air valves are opened and ram air is used to cool the same equipment areas that were previously cooled under normal operation except for the nose radar equipment which is automatically switched OFF. The cockpit air supply valve remains closed to altitude may have to be reduced as any further pressurization of the cabin will cease. Cabin pressure will fall at the natural leakage rate of the cabin.

(d)   A two position switch marked CABIN PRESS and DUMP. The switch must be in the CABIN PRESS position for cabin pressurization to take place. In the DUMP position the cabin safety valve is opened and any pressure existing at the time is discharged through the valve; no further cabin pressurization will take place with the switch in this position. Air conditioning of the armament bay ceases when the DUMP selection is made.

(e)   A toggle switch marked TEMP CONTROL-EMERG OFF. When selected to EMERG OFF this switch shuts off the supply of hot air to the cabin and the equipment areas. Cool air continues to flow to provide cabin pressurization and equipment cooling.

Safety Provisions in the System

105.   Should the cooling turbine outlet temperature exceed 80°F, the AIR COND FAIL warning light will illuminate. (See para 104.)

106.   Should the temperature of the supply air to the equipment areas exceed 100°F, the hot air supply in these areas is automatically cut off and the EQUIP O'HEAT warning light will illuminate. (See para 104).

107.   The hot air valve of the cabin air supply will automatically close if the temperature of the air to the cockpits reaches 240°F. The valve will open again when the temperature has decreased to 100°F.

108.   Two red warning lights are fitted above a three way toggle switch on the forward RH console. The lights are marked ENG BLEED, and arrows indicate their particular engine. The

switch is marked ENG BLEED AIR, with three positions LH OFF-NORMAL-RH OFF. A particular ENG BLEED light will illuminate should a leakage of engine bleed hot air occur in the ducting to the air-to-air heat exchanger, or should the bleed air reach an excessive pressure through failure of a pressure reducing valve. Selecting the switch to the appropriate side indicated by the warning light (i.e. LH OFF or RH OFF), will close the shut-off valve in the engine bleed air supply duct on that side. If the condition is relieved, the warning light will go out.

NOTE

Red lights are used as no master warning light illuminates.

Single Engine Flying

109.   If one engine is shut down, or a drop in pressure of the engine bleed air to the heat exchanger occurs for any reason, a pressure switch is operated and a signal shuts off the electronic equipment in the nose compartment. (Aircraft with radar fitted.)

System Operation with Landing Gear Down

110.   When the landing gear is lowered, a switch operated by the main door uplock is actuated. This action almost closes the cockpit air shut-off valve to conserve the air supply. Flaps in the ram air ducts are also opened when the landing gear is lowered to connect the turbine fan inlet with the ram air intakes.

COCKPIT CANOPIES

General

111.   The front and rear cockpits each have an independently operated two-piece canopy. Each canopy is normally opened or closed by electrical actuators controlled by switches, and is locked or unlocked manually by a lever which operates latches.

112.   Power for canopy actuation is supplied from the battery bus so that opening or closing can be carried out when the master electrical switch is off.

NOTE

The canopies should only be opened or closed once during a flight cycle when using the aircraft battery. If more than one operation is required and provided the engines have not been started, a starting cart or ground supply should be used. This will prevent excessive drain on the aircraft battery.

113.   Provision is made to open the canopy in an emergency by means of gas generating cartridges which may be fired either from inside or outside the aircraft. In case of seat ejection, a canopy is opened and the seat is ejected by pulling a large overhead firing handle down over the face, or alternatively by pulling the alternative fire handle on the seat pan. (See para 216.)

Normal Operation

114.   A switch marked CANOPY/OPEN-OFF-CLOSE is located in each cockpit n the LH console and controls the operation of the canopy for that cockpit. The switches are spring loaded to OFF and must be held in the required position until the operation is completed. The canopy locking lever must be fully back before the canopy open-close switch is operative.

115.   When the canopy has been fully closed by the switch, it is locked by means of an overhead lever which is pushed fully forward manually by the cockpit occupant. Pulling down and moving the lever to the first detent will latch or lock the two halves of the canopy together. It must then be pulled down and moved fully forward. It will engage a switch and, provided the other canopy is closed and locked, will operate the canopy seal pressurization valve and inflate the seals of both canopies. When a canopy is locked, the canopy open-close switch is de-energized and is inoperative. The lever is held in the fully forward position by a spring loaded plunger.

116.   The canopy is opened when the aircraft is on the ground by pulling the overhead lever down and fully to the rear. The first rearward movement of the lever will deflate the seal of both canopies. As the lever passes the first detent position it unlocks the two halves of the canopy. When the lever is fully back the canopy open-close switch is energized and holding this switch in the open position will fully open the canopy.

Normal Operation from the Ground

117.   The canopies may be opened or closed from outside the aircraft by means of two switches, one for each canopy, fitted on the canopy arch. The switches are marked CANOPIES/OPEN-OFF-CLOSE and are spring loaded to OFF. If a canopy is locked, then that particular switch is de-energized and is non-operative.

Emergency Opening from the Ground

118.   If the canopies are locked, the CANOPY OPEN-CLOSE switches outside the aircraft are inoperative. In an emergency the canopy locks can be released and the canopies opened by gas cartridge pressure.

119.   An access door located on the RH side of the aircraft nose below the pilot's cockpit, marked EMERGENCY CANOPY OPENING must be opened. Located inside is a lanyard, which is attached to the canopy emergency opening lever in both front and rear cockpits. Pulling this lanyard down moves the emergency levers in both cockpits and fires gas generating cartridges. Gas pressure is released which first unlocks the canopy locking levers and then operates the emergency jacks, which open the canopies. When the emergency jacks are operated a shear pin on the electrically actuated jacks is sheared. When opened by this method the canopies open slightly more than for normal opening.

Emergency Opening in the Air

120.   Each canopy may be opened individually in an emergency when in flight by operation of the emergency lever fitted on the RH side of each cockpit.

121.   After an emergency canopy opening lever has been pulled, the operation of the gas generator and jacks is the same as in para 119.

NOTE

When a canopy is opened by the cartridge operated system the electrically operated jack is sheared, preventing closing of the canopy.

122.   If the emergency canopy opening system fails to function, the canopies may be opened over a limited speed range by the normal operating jacks controlled by the CANOPY OPEN-CLOSE switches. Further information will be issued later.

LIGHTING EQUIPMENT

Cockpit Lights

123.   A panel, marked COCKPIT LIGHTING, is located on the RH console in both front and rear cockpits. A toggle switch and three rheostat switches are fitted on each panel to control the lighting. An emergency flood and map light, powered from the DC emergency bus, is provided on the RH side of each cockpit and is controlled by a press switch on the light. The individual switches on the panel control are as follows:

(a)   A rheostat switch marked MAIN PANEL-OFF/BRIGHT, controls the main instrument panel red instrument lights. Power is taken from the main AC bus.

(b)   A rheostat switch marked CONSOLE PANELS-OFF/BRIGHT controls the red edge lights for the console panels and main instrument panel. Power is taken from the main AC bus.

(c)   A rheostat switch marked CONSOLE FLOOD-OFF/BRIGHT controls the red console flood lights. Power is taken from the main AC bus.

(d)   A toggle switch marked HIGH ALT LIGHTING-ON/OFF controls the amber flood lights for the main instrument panel and consoles. Power is taken from the main DC bus.

External Lights

124.   External lights comprise two landing/taxi lights, and the navigation lights. The landing lights are fitted on the nose landing gear. One is fitted on the steering portion for taxiing purposes and the other is fitted on the fixed portion of the leg. A switch, fitted on the LH console, in the front cockpit and marked LIGHTS, has three positions, LAND-TAXI-OFF. With the landing gear extended, selection of LAND will illuminate both lights while selection of TAXI will allow only the taxi light to illuminate. (Landing and taxi lights are not fitted for the first flights of the first aircraft.)

125.   The navigation lights consist of the right (green) and left (red) wing tip lights and two fin tip lights (white and red). They are controlled by a flasher unit through a switch located on the RH forward console in the front cockpit marked NAV LIGHTS/FLASH-OFF-STEADY. When selected to FLASH the two wing tip lights and the white fin tip light will be on together and will flash alternately with the red fin tip light. The lights will revert to 'steady' should the flasher unit fail.

ENGINE CONTROLS

Engine Power Controls

126.   Two conventionally operated engine throttle levers are installed on the LH console. Movement of each lever operates the fuel flow control quadrant lever at the engine via a continuous cable. The cable is automatically maintained at correct tension by a tension regulating device.

127.   Each lever has "gated" stops to enable a positive selection of the cut-off and idle positions. Lifting and pulling the levers aft of the idle position shuts off the HP fuel supply to the engines. To move the levers from the cut-off to the idle position they must be moved forwards and down.

Afterburner Control

128.   Each throttle lever controls non-afterburning and afterburning engine operation as follows:

(a)   Progressive forward movement of the lever up to the maximum stop position selects a range of engine thrust (without afterburning) from "idle" to "military" power.

(b)   Progressive forward movement from "idle" to a position marked DOWN

FOR AFTERBURNER on the quadrant gives normal engine thrust. Depression of the lever within the afterburner range actuates a micro-switch and the afterburner lights. Engine and afterburner thrust increases progressively as the lever is moved forward to the maximum stop position.

129.   Afterburning can be terminated immediately by lifting the lever to the original 'up' position within the quadrant. This relieves the pressure on the micro-switch which cuts off the afterburner.

130.   Should a failure of the electrical system occur during afterburner operation, the afterburner may be shut down by retarding the throttle lever out of the afterburner range. This actuates a hydro-mechanical device within the flow-control unit. The afterburner cannot be used again until the electrical fault has been rectified.

Engine Starting Controls

131.   The engine starting controls comprise:

(a)   An ENGINE START switch with START-OFF-RESET positions, located on the RH console.

(b)   A relight button on each throttle lever.

(c)   An LP FUEL cock switch for each engine, located on the LH console.

(d)   An HP fuel cock for each engine controlled by its respective throttle lever.

132.   During the normal start procedure when the ENGINE START switch is pulsed to START and released, the following sequence of operations automatically take place:

(a)   A switch is operated in the air turbine starter motor when the engine reaches approximately 700 rpm which energizes the ignition circuit for "light-up".

(b)   A second switch in the air turbine starter motor is operated when the engine reaches approximately 3,000 rpm, and performs the following operations simultaneously:

(1)   Switches off the ignition.

(2)   Shuts off the air supply from the ground starter cart.

Engine Motoring

133.   The engines may be motored should a wet start occur, or in the case of an internal engine fire on the ground, as follows:

(a)   Move the throttle lever to the cut-off position.

(b)   Check that the LP cocks are in the ON Position.

(c)   Air starting power must be available from the ground starter unit.

(d)   Select the ENGINE START switch to the RESET position an hold for a maximum time limit of 30 seconds. Allow the switch to return to the OFF position. The engine will motor at approximately 1,200 rpm.

NOTE

Holding the ENGINE START switch to the RESET position immediately isolates the ignition circuit, opens the air supply valve in the ground starter unit and permits the engine to rotate. When the switch is released, the air supply valve in the ground starter unit is closed and the engine will gradually run down.

ENGINE INSTRUMENTS

Pressure Ratio Indicator

134.   An Engine Pressure Ratio Indicator for each engine is fitted on the main instrument panel. Each indicator denotes the ratio of the turbine discharge total pressure to the compressor inlet total pressure and is an indication of the power being developed by each engine.

135.   The ratio shown on the indicator for an engine developing military thrust at take-off will vary from day to day, according to the ambient temperature.

136.   To compute the engine pressure ratio which is normally functioning engine may be expected to produce during a take-off thrust check, a curve as shown in the engine operating handbook may be used. This curve for the ARROW I installation will be issued later.

137.   Curves may be used for determining the engine pressure ratio for a desired engine power setting, either for a climb or cruise condition, the factors involved being altitude and compressor inlet total temperature (ambient temperature corrected for ram effect). This curve will also be issued later.

138.   Once the desired power condition has been set up for climb or cruise, the fuel control will maintain an approximate constant percentage of thrust output with a fixed power lever position. As engine pressure ratio varies with compressor inlet temperature, the pressure ratio will increase as the temperature becomes lower at the higher altitudes.

Engine RPM Indicator

139.   An rpm indicator (tachometer) graduated in percentage rpm, is fitted on the main instrument panel for each engine. On the indicator 100% rpm represents a high pressure compressor speed of 8732 rpm.

NOTE

The low pressure compressor rpm are not instrumented on this aircraft.

140.   The 100% position is not the rpm at which Military Rated thrust will be developed by the engine. The rpm for military rated thrust on standard day sea level static conditions for different engines will vary, depending upon the engine trim speed which is stamped on the engine data plate. The rpm serves as an indication that compressor speed is within allowable limits. A red line on the indicator at 103.5% represents the overspeed limit.

CAUTION

Each case of rpm overspeed in excess of 103.5% should be noted in the engine log book.

141.   The rpm indicators can be used for checking engine power output. In this case, temperature/rpm curves must be used and the result adjusted for the particular engine trim speed.

Turbine Outlet Temperature Gauge

142.   One gauge is fitted for each engine, indicating the temperature immediately downstream from the turbine discharge and serving as a relative indication of the temperature at the turbine inlet. The instruments require AC power. Two flags are visible at windows on the face of the instrument. When electrical power is off, both flags show the word OFF. When electrical power is ON, the flags disappear. One flag is always visible in the event of the other flag being obscured by the indicating pointer.

LOW PRESSURE PNEUMATIC SYSTEM

General

143.   The LP pneumatic system supplies low pressure air, tapped from the inlet side of the air conditioning cooling turbine, to the anti-g suits and the canopy seals.

Anti-g Suit Controls

144.   An anti-g valve is located at the aft end of the RH console in each cockpit and controls the LP air supply to the anti-g suit. The valves are set to pressurize the suits at 1.5 g - 1.8 g. the pressurization will increase with the increase of "g" forces up to a maximum of approximately 10 psig which would be reached at 8 g. If 8 g is exceeded the suit will not pressurize above 10 psig. Connection between anti-g valve and anti-g suit is made through the crew member's composite leads disconnect on the RH side of the seat pan.

Canopy Seals

145.   The pilot's and navigator's canopy seals are inflated by low pressure air at 18-22 psi through a control valve. The valve is operated electrically and the seals are inflated when both canopy handles are in the locked position. If either canopy is unlocked the seals will deflate and vent the pressure to atmosphere. The rear cockpit canopy locking handle may be operated from the front cockpit through an access door in the bulkhead, to enable the rear canopy to be locked if the aircraft is flown solo.

DE-ICING AND ANTI-ICING SYSTEMS

General

146.   The aircraft anti-icing and de-icing systems are entirely automatic in operation. The engine systems may be divided as follows:

(a)   Ice detection.

(b)   De-icing of the duct intake ramps and lips. (Non-operative for the first flights of the first aircraft.)

(c)   Engine compressor inlet anti-icing. (Non-operative for the first flights of the aircraft.)

147.   The airframe systems are as follows:

(a)   Windscreen and canopy anti-icing.

(b)   Pitot head anti-icing.

(c)   Probe vane anti-icing.

Ice Detection

148.   Two identical electrically heated ice detectors are fitted; one mounted on the lip of each engine intake duct.

149.   Each detector has two probes, one of which is electrically heated whenever power is ON, and the other which is only heated when ice covers the forward holes. A pressure differential switch signals the ice controller when ice forms on the normally unheated probe. The signal also causes the master amber warning light and the light on the warning panel, marked ICE, to illuminate. The automatic heating of this probe melts the ice on the probe, restores the normal pressure, and the probe is then ready to send another signal to the ice controller. The signals continue as long as icing conditions exist, at a rate proportional to the rate of icing. The rate is indicated to the pilot by the ICE warning light and the master amber light, going on and off.

Duct De-icing

150.   De-icing of the engine ducts is accomplished by electrically heated rubber ice protectors which are automatically controlled. The protectors are separated by parting strips which are heated at the first ice signal from the controller (para 149). The remainder of the protectors are heated after a pre-set number of ice signals are received and will shed the ice. The icing and de-icing cycle will be repeated according to the number of signals received by the controller.

Engine Compressor Inlet Anti-icing

151.   Engine anti-icing is accomplished by the use of engine bleed air. The first icing signal from the controller automatically opens air supply valves and provides hot air to the compressor inlet section of the engine. The system functions continuously during icing conditions. The valves close automatically at the same time as the duct de-icing ceases.

152.   The flow of hot air is regulated according to the compressor discharge temperature. Flow will be reduced as the temperature increases.

NOTE

During descent at high airspeeds and low power settings the heat supplied may be inadequate if the ice formation is severe. Increased thrust should be applied to provide more heat. An abnormal increase in turbine discharge temperature will be noted when the throttles are advanced if ice is still accumulating in the compressor inlet. Airspeed should be decreased until the icing region has been passed.

Windscreen and Canopy Anti-Icing

153.   The pilot's windscreen and canopy windows are continuously heated by electrical means when the aircraft master electrical switch is on. A conductive transparent coating is incorporated on the inner surface of the outer glass lamination of the panels and sensing elements control the maximum temperature to 110°F.

Pitot-head and Vane Anti-Icing

154.   The pitot-heads and probe vanes are continuously heated by electrical means when the aircraft master electrical switch is on.

OXYGEN SYSTEM

General

155.   Two independent oxygen systems are installed in the aircraft, a normal supply and an emergency supply.

Normal System

156.   The normal system is supplied from a converter containing liquid oxygen. The liquid oxygen is converted into gaseous oxygen for crew members breathing purposes and, on later aircraft, for inflation of the partial pressure suits.

157.   The quantity of liquid oxygen contained in the converter is shown on two gauges in litres. One gauge is fitted on the forward RH console in the pilot's cockpit, while the other gauge is fitted on the navigator's main panel. The gauges are operated electrically and, on later aircraft, an OFF indicator flag on each gauge becomes visible when electrical power to the quantity gauging system is terminated.

158.   Oxygen flows from the converter, through the composite leads disconnect to a regulator which automatically compensates for altitude. From the regulator it flows back to the composite leads disconnect, from which leads are taken to the oxygen mask and pressure suit.

Oxygen Regulator

159.   An automatic pressure demand oxygen regulator is fitted beneath each seat pan. A PRESS-TO-TEST button is fitted on the right of the seat pan and is used to test the mask prior to flight.

Emergency Oxygen Supply

160.   Attached to the forward part of each seat pan is an emergency oxygen cylinder containing gaseous oxygen at a pressure of 180 psi when fully charged. The oxygen pressure is shown on a gauge attached to the cylinder. A fully charged cylinder provides a minimum of 20 minutes supply.

161.   A combined automatic and manual trip valve is fitted to each cylinder. The automatic function operates upon seat ejection by means of a lanyard, which connects the valve to the floor of the aircraft. Should the normal oxygen supply fail, the emergency bottle supply may be used by operating the EMERGENCY OXYGEN MANUAL CONTROL located on the LH side of each seat pan. In both automatic or manual function, the trip valve connects the emergency cylinder

to the regulator, and to the mask and pressure suit through the composite leads disconnect. Thus the regulator adjusts the emergency supply in the same manner as the normal supply is adjusted.

Composite Leads Disconnect

162.   A composite leads disconnect fitting is located on the right of each ejection seat pan. Connections from the fitting are as follows:

(a)   Oxygen to mask and pressure to suit. (Not connected to the suit in the first aircraft.)

(b)   Telecommunications.

(c)   Anti-g suit.

163.   The fitting is in three parts and when seat ejection takes place one part of the fitting remains with the aircraft while the other two parts are attached to the seat. This allows emergency oxygen to be used during the early part of the descent. When the occupant separates from the seat, the remaining two parts disconnect, leaving one on the seat and the other attached to the occupant.

UTILITY HYDRAULIC SYSTEM

General

164.   The utility hydraulic system is separate from the flying control hydraulic system. The utility system is powered by two pumps, one mounted on each engine driven gear box. An operating pressure of 4000 psi is maintained by the pumps. Any one pump will supply the requirements of the utility hydraulic sub-systems.

165.   A 5000 psi nitrogen charged storage bottle is provided for emergency extension of the landing gear. Two 4000 psi accumulators are included in the system for emergency braking.

166.   The utility hydraulic system operates the following components:

(a)   Landing gear.

(b)   Wheel brakes.

(c)   Nose Wheel steering.

(d)   Speed brakes.

(e)   A hydraulic motor to drive the emergency alternator. Operation is automatic in case of complete electrical failure.

(f)   A hydraulic jack for extending a ram air driven turbine into the airstream to give flying control hydraulic pressure in an emergency. (If fitted.)

Landing Gear

167.   The tricycle landing gear consists of a forward retracting nose gear with dual wheels and main gears with two wheeled bogies which retract inboard and forward into the wing.

Landing Gear Controls

168.   The landing gear is operated by means of a lever which has a wheel shaped handle containing a red light, located on the landing gear selector panel on the LH forward panel.

169.   A solenoid operated micro-switch prevents raising of the landing gear while the weight of the aircraft is on the main wheels. No provision is made for emergency retraction of the landing gear.

Emergency Lowering Landing Gear

170.   In the event of failure of the normal system, the landing gear may be lowered by means of pneumatic pressure from a 5000 psi nitrogen storage bottle. To operate the system a thumb latch marked EMERGENCY EXTENSION, under the landing gear lever is pressed down and the lever is moved fully downwards. The pneumatic pressure releases the uplocks of the doors and gears at approximately the same time, and each gear then falls in a manner similar to normal lowering.

Landing Gear Position Indicators

171.   Three indicators marked GEAR POSITION are located on the LH side of the main instrument panel, and show the position of the two main gears and nose gear. In addition, a red light is fitted into the handle of the landing gear selector lever and illuminates steadily when any gear or gear doors are between locks. The red light flashes if either throttle lever is retarded below the minimum cruise position if the landing gear selector lever is not in the down position. When the throttle of a non-operating engine is placed in the cut-off position for one engine flight, the light will go out. However, the light will illuminate again when the throttle lever of the live engine is retarded if the landing gear lever has not been selected down.

172.   With electrical power switched on, the three indicators on the main panel show landing gear position as follows:

Position	Indication	Landing Gear Handle Warning Light
Landing Gear and Doors Locked Up	UP	OFF
Landing Gear or Doors Between Locks	Black and White bars	ON
Landing Gear and Doors Locked Down	Wheel symbol	OFF

Sequencing of Landing Gear and Doors

173.   When the landing gear lever is moved UP after take-off the individual indicators will show diagonal bars as the gear down-locks are released by hydraulic pressure. At the same time the red light in the handle of the gear lever will illuminate. As the individual gear nears its uplock position in the wheel bay, a valve is operated causing the door downlock to be released and the door to be closed. As each door closes a micro-switch is tripped, which causes an UP signal to show on the indicator for that particular gear. When all three doors are closed,the red warning light on the landing gear lever handle goes out. The selector valve (which is moved by electrical means whenever the landing gear lever is moved) is automatically returned to neutral. This allows the emergency extension system to be used in case an electrical failure causes the selector valve to be inoperative.

174.   If one door becomes unlocked during flight and releases its micro-switch plunger, the red light will illuminate in the landing gear selector lever handle and the gear position indicator will show diagonal bars (gear unsafe). At the same time power will be applied to the UP solenoid of the selector valve, the door will be retracted, the indicator will show UP and the lever handle light will go out. The selector valve will again automatically return to neutral.

175.   When the landing gear is selected DOWN, hydraulic pressure releases the door and gear uplocks in sequence and the gear falls by gravity aided by air loads. Its fall is restricted by a fixed orifice in the jack and is damped at the final portion of extension. The red light in the gear handle will illuminate and remain illuminated until the gears and doors are locked down. The indicator travels through the stages from up, unlocked to locked down.

Wheel Brakes

176.   Toe pressure on the pilot's rudder brake pedals actuates control valves via cables and allows differential and proportional braking of the two pairs of main wheels. No anti-skid protection is provided on early aircraft, but later aircraft will be fitted with an anti-skid system which will release pressure on the brakes when a skid is imminent.

177.   Brakes are applied automatically upon retraction of the landing gear to stop the wheels spinning. An emergency braking system automatically provides differential and proportional braking in the event of failure of the normal system.

Anti-skid System (Not fitted on early aircraft)

178.   Detection of an imminent skid of a wheel and immediate release of pressure to that brake to prevent actual skidding, is provided on later aircraft. To prevent excessive differential braking being used when the pressure is cut off from one side, the other side brake is also released, thus preventing a yawing effect.

179.   A locked-wheel touchdown is prevented by a micro-switch which prevents brakes being used until the weight of the aircraft is on the main wheels. Detectors are also fitted which prevent use of the brakes until the wheels are rotating at the aircraft landing speed.

180.   In case of failure of an anti-skid unit, selecting the ANTI-SKID switch located on the LH console to EMERG OFF disconnects all anti-skid units.

Brake Pressures

181.   The normal utility system pressure of 4000 psi is supplied to the master brake cylinder, where it is reduced to 2500 psi. Emergency pressure is supplied to the brake control valve at 1500 psi which is sufficient for adequate braking. The emergency accumulators are maintained at a pressure of 4000 psi by the main system.

Pressure Warning Lights

182.   If the pressure in the normal utility system falls below 1000 psi, the master amber warning light and the UTIL HYD indicator light on the warning panel, will illuminate. This indicates that emergency extension of the landing gear will be necessary and that emergency brake pressure will be used for braking upon landing. Should the pressure in the emergency accumulators fall below 1600 psi, the EMERG BRAKE HYD indicator light on the warning panel will illuminate and indicate that emergency braking will be inoperative upon landing.

Parking Brake

183.   A handle is fitted on the LH side of the main instrument panel and is marked PARKING. The brakes can be locked on for parking by depressing the rudder brake pedals, pulling the parking brake control and releasing the brakes. To release the parking brakes, the handle is pulled outwards and allowed to return fully inwards.

184.   The emergency accumulator provides hydraulic pressure for the brakes when towing the aircraft or for parking after engine shut-down.

Nose Wheel Steering

185.   The nose wheels are steered hydraulically by the movement of the pilot's rudder pedals which are mechanically linked to the steering control valve. A solenoid valve is opened when the push button, located at the bottom left of the control column grip, is pressed. This allows high pressure hydraulic fluid to flow to the control valve which operates a jack and moves the nose wheel according to the pilot's rudder pedal movements. When the nose wheel reaches an angle corresponding to the position of the rudder pedals, the control valve spool returns to normal. The rudder pedal position must be synchronized with the nose wheel position when initiating steering. Normal castoring of the nose wheels is available when steering is not engaged. A micro-switch prevents turning of the nose wheels unless the weight of the aircraft is on the nose wheels.

Steering Angles

186.   The nose wheels can be steered or castored through an angle of 55" on either side of the centre line, enabling the aircraft to be turned on a 21 foot radius.

Speed Brakes

187.   Two speed brakes are fitted in the bottom of the fuselage immediately aft of the armament bay. They are hydraulically operated by the utilities system and are controlled by a thumb switch on the RH throttle lever. The switch opens or closes the electrical circuit to a solenoid operated hydraulic control valve. The speed brakes are designed to open and "hold" at speeds up to Mach 1.0. They will "blow in" to a new position if excessive air loads are imposed, until airloads balance the hydraulic jack load.

Selector Switch

188.   The speed brake selector switch has three positions, fully forward - "OUT", central - "HOLD", and fully back -"IN". The switch should remain at the IN position when speed brakes are not in use and at the OUT position when using them fully down. The 'hold' position may be used to obtain intermediate selections, the speed brakes being hydraulically locked in the position existing at the time of selection.

NAVIGATION EQUIPMENT

Radio Magnetic Indicator

189.   The pilot and navigator are each supplied with a RADIO MAGNETIC INDICATOR, located on their respective main instrument panels. A selector switch, marked RMI NEEDLE - UHF HOMER/TACAN is fitted in both cockpits on the RH console. Provided an individual switch is selected to TACAN, (if TACAN is fitted) the double pointer of the radio magnetic indicator in that particular cockpit will show the relative bearing of the selected beacon station. With the switch selected to UHF HOMER the same pointer will indicate the relative bearing of the station selected on the ARC-34 receiver. The compass card of the RMI is controlled by the J4 compass and indicates the magnetic heading of the aircraft. (See J4 Compass.) The single pointer is used, in conjunction with the radio compass, to obtain a bearing of a broadcast or radio range station. (See Radio Compass).

UHF Homer

190.   This navigational aid utilizes the AN/ARC-34 main receiver (see Communication Equipment). Homing facilities are provided by selecting the OFF-MAIN-BOTH-ADF switch on the COMM control panel to ADF. Provided the RMI NEEDLE selector switch on the RH console is selected to UHF HOMER, the double pointer of the RMI will indicate the relative bearing of the selected radio signal source, and enable the aircraft to "home" on the signal. Signals must be in the 225 to 400 MC range for automatic direction finding to operate. Successful operation depends upon the power of the transmitting station, the altitude and the distance between the transmitting station and the aircraft. Results will not be dependable if the horizon appears between the transmitting station and the aircraft.

Radio Compass (AN/ARN-6 L.F)

191.   The ARN-6 radio compass receiver provides a bearing on broadcast or radio range stations, and the relative bearing is shown by the single pointer on the radio magnetic indicators. A RADIO COMPASS control panel is fitted on the RH console in both cockpits, but only one panel is in control at a time. The tuning dial of the control panel in use is illuminated. Control may be gained by the other crew member by turning the selector switch to CONT (control) and then back to COMP. The bearing indication is shown on the single pointers of both radio magnetic indicators simultaneously. Audio signals are received through the AN/AIC 10 interphone system, provided the mixing switch on the interphone panel marked COMP, is ON.

192.   A station is tuned by means of a band selector switch and a tuning knob. Mode of operation is selected as follows:

COMP -   To obtain station bearing automatically.

ANT   -   To operate as a communications receiver only.

COMP -   To obtain bearing manually by means of a loop drive control on the panel.

J4 Gyrosyn Compass

193.   A remote compass transmitter is installed in the right wing and magnetic heading information is transmitted to the cards of the radio magnetic indicators and the R-Theta computer system (if fitted). A J4 compass control panel is fitted on the RH console in the pilot's cockpit and the following controls are installed:

(a)   A function selector switch marked MAG-DG is used to select the mode of operation of the compass system. When the switch is in the MAG (magnetic) position, the system operates as a magnetic compass and can by synchronized with the remote transmitter. In the DG (directional gyro) position, the system operates as a directional gyro, which can be latitude corrected.

(b)   A synchronizer knob marked SET, which is spring loaded to the SET position. The knob may be moved to the left (marked DECR-) or to the right (marked INCR+) in order to line up the annunciator pointer with the centre index when the function selector is in the MAG position. When the selector is in the DG position the annunciator window is covered and the letters DG appear. The synchronizing knob may be moved to INCR or DECR to set the indicators to the desired position at either a fast or slow rate.

(c)   The latitude correction controller, marked LAT is manually set to the flight latitude to correct the system, when in the DG mode of operation, for the apparent drift of the gyro due to the earth's rotation.

(d)   A hemisphere screw adjustment marked N and S is normally set on the ground to the northern or southern hemisphere in which the gyro is operated. Setting it to "N" will effect a clockwise correction for gyro drift, while an "S" setting will effect a counter-clockwise correction; the rate of precession is determined by the setting of the latitude correction controller.

(e)   An annunciator which indicates synchronization to ± 15' between the compass system and the remote transmitter when in the magnetic mode of operation. When the system is not synchronized, the annunciator indicates in which direction the synchronizer knob must be turned.

194.   A J4 COMP NORMAL-AEROBATICS switch is fitted on a panel located below the radio compass control panel, on the pilot's RH console. If violent manoeuvres are to be carried out the switch should be selected to AEROBATICS to cage the compass gyro and prevent toppling. Selection back to NORMAL should be made after the aircraft has returned to normal flight.

R-Theta Navigation Computer System (Not fitted at the present time.)

195.   The R-Theta system is a dead reckoning method of navigation which supplies the aircraft's ground position in the form of range and bearing from base or destination. The aircraft's true track is also indicated. Interception steering information can also be shown.

196.   True airspeed and magnetic heading enter the Ground Speed Computer as electrical signals and variation, wind speed and direction are fed in manually by the navigator. The Ground Speed Computer carries out a continuous solution of the triangle of velocities; that is, it performs the addition of air speed and wind speed vectors and taking into account magnetic variation, extracts ground speed and true track data. These are transmitted to the R-Theta computer as electrical signals. The R-Theta DR computer processes true track and ground speed data with respect to time so as to determine continuously the aircraft's ground position, and displays range, true bearing and true track. Controls for adding arbitrary vectors, and for resetting range and gearing are located on the face of the navigator's computer.

197.   Instruments used by the pilot and navigator are as follows:

(a)   A Ground Speed and Interception Computer used by the navigator.

(b)   An R-Theta DR Computer used by the navigator.

(c)   An R-Theta DR Indicator used by the pilot, which is a repeater from the navigator's computer.

198.   The G.S.I.C. enables the basic variables of magnetic or grid variation, windspeed and wind direction to be set by the three manual controls, with a corresponding indication on the dials and counters. The aircraft's true airspeed is automatically indicated on the cut out window. The above information when set on the G.S.I.C., plus information fed from the J4 gyro compass, enables the R-Theta computer to carry out the functions set out below.

199.   The R-Theta computer shows the true bearing of the aircraft from a chosen reference point, with the double arrows always pointing towards this point. The single pointer indicates the aircraft's true track. The range counter automatically indicates the aircraft's distance in nautical miles from a chosen reference point.

200.   The pilot's repeater displays the same range, bearing and track data as the navigator's computer. A switch on the repeater instrument permits the selection of compass heading or true heading as alternatives to true track.

COMMUNICATION EQUIPMENT

UHF Equipment (AN/ARC-34)

201.   An AN/ARC-34 receiver-transmitter is installed and permits short range voice transmission and reception, air-to-air or ground, on 20 preset channels. Any other channel within the operating range may be selected manually. Reception and transmission is made through the AIC/10 interphone system. The control panel, marked COMM, is located on the console in the pilot's cockpit and comprises:

(a)   An OFF-MAIN-BOTH-ADF switch, which sets up the type of operation as follows:

OFF.

MAIN -   Main transmitter/receiver is operative.
BOTH -   Main transmitter/receiver and the Guard receiver are both operative.
ADF   -   The automatic direction finder (HOMER) is operative.
       (See NAVIGATION EQUIPMENT - UHF HOMER.)

(b)   A MANUAL/PRESET/GUARD switch which selects the type of frequency control for the transmitter and main receiver. When PRESET is selected, the large central knob is rotated to bring the required channel number in the centre window. The preset channel numbers are inscribed on a card at the base of the panel. When MANUAL is selected, four windows at the top of the panel open and expose digits, which may be altered to the frequency required by means of a knob located below each window. When GUARD is selected the windows are closed and the transmitter and main receiver operate on the GUARD frequency.

(c)   A TONE button, which provides MCW transmission.

(d)   A VOLUME control.

202.   Two antennas are fitted for the UHF equipment, one in the fin and one in the equipment bay. They are known as upper and lower respectively, and may be selected at the pilot's discretion by means of a two position switch on the RH console in the front cockpit. The switch is marked UHF ANT-UPPER/LOWER.

Intercommunication (AN/AIC-10)

203.   Intercommunication is provided by an AN/AIC-10 set. It provides interphone between aircrew, ground crew and operations room and also affords a means of selection of the aircraft's radio facilities.

204.   Identical control boxes are fitted for the pilot and the navigator and are located on their respective RH consoles. A PRESS-TO-TALK button is fitted on the RH throttle lever in the front cockpit and on the panel forward of the AIC-10 panel in the rear cockpit. The control box comprises the following switches:

(a)   A series of five mixing toggle switches which allow for listening simultaneously on all channels which are selected to the ON position.

Switch 1 marked INTER - For interphone between pilot and navigator.
Switch 2 marked COMP - Radio Compass AN/ARN-6 aural reception, used to tune and identify a particular station.
Switch 3 marked COMM - Command radio, gives UHF reception to other aircraft or ground stations.
Switch 4 marked TACAN - AN/ARN-21 radio set aural reception used to tune and identify a particular station.
Switch 5 marked TEL - For telescramble information reception when the aircraft is on the ground.

(b)   A six position rotary switch giving talk facilities by means of the following selections:

Position 1 - (Fully counter-clockwise) - Spare.
Position 2 - Spare.
Position 3 - Marked TEL, provides transmission facilities through the telescramble line when the aircraft is on the ground by operating on "Press to Transmit" button.
Position 4 - Marked COMM. Provides a "live" microphone for interphone without interrupting command radio listening, provided the INTER mixing switch is ON. When the "Press to Talk" button is pressed, it permits transmission of command radio.
Position 5 - Marked INTER. Provides "Press to Talk" interphone operation.
Position 6 - Marked CALL. Spring loaded in the fully clockwise position and returns to position 5 (INTER) when released. When held in the CALL position it overrides all other functions irrespective of switch positions and gives interphone without the use of the "Press to Talk" button.

205.   The "Press to Talk" button is used when the selector switch is in the COMM position and it is desired to transmit on command radio or in the TEL position when transmitting on the telescramble line. When the selector switch is in the INTER position "Press to Talk" interphone facilities are available regardless of the mixing switch positions. A volume control is fitted and adjusts volume on all incoming channels.

206.   A toggle switch marked NORMAL-AUX. LISTEN is wire-locked in the NORMAL position, but if reception at the station fails a quick test of the amplifier may be made by breaking the locking wire and listening with the switch on AUX. LISTEN; this cuts out the amplifier. This facility is available for emergency listening in flight, and when used, the mixing is inoperative and one channel only is available for listening, as selected by a toggle switch. If more than one switch is on, the only audible channel will be that given by the first (from the left) of the row of mixing switches that are on. If none are ON, the only audible channel will be the one to which the rotary selector switch is set.

207.   Inadvertent rotation of the selector switch past the TEL position will result in interruption of the talk facility.

208.   Numerous combinations of switch positions are possible. One example is given below:

(a)   Mixing switches on INTER and COMM.

(b)   Rotary switch on COMM.

(c)   Volume control with the white line at approximately the mid position.

209.   Under the above arrangement interphone, both with navigator and ground crew, is available at all times without any other operation, command radio is available for listening; and by pressing the"Press to Talk" button, transmission on command radio is available.

NOTE

The above position of the volume control will provide maximum efficiency. Movement past this position may be used for reception during abnormal atmospheric conditions or weak signal strength. The volume of the UHF and radio compass should then be adjusted individually as desired.

OPERATIONAL EQUIPMENT AND CONTROLS

IFF (AN/APX-6A)

210.   The purpose of the IFF equipment is to enable the aircraft in which it is installed to identify itself when interrogated by coded trans-missions from ground or airborne radar sets. The coded interrogation transmissions can be transmitted in any one of three modes classified as Modes 1, 2 and 3. Each mode of interrogation initiates the transmission of a corresponding mode of reply from the IFF transmitter-receiver (transponder). The reply is presented on the interrogator's radar display adjacent to the target pip.

211.   Mode 1 interrogation serves for general identification of any aircraft detected by a ground or airborne radar set. Modes 2 and 3 permit specific aircraft to be identified and distinguished from other aircraft. Normally, Modes 2 and 3 are used only when requested by radio or prior to take-off.

212.   An emergency reply, which overrides the three normal modes can be selected. This reply will be transmitted when the aircraft is interrogated irrespective of the mode of interrogation.

213.   The control panel is located on the LH console in the pilot's cockpit and comprises the following control switches:

(a)   MASTER switch - A five position rotary switch used to control power supplies to the equipment and to select EMERGENCY operation. The switch positions are as follows:

(1)   OFF: All power supplies are disconnected from the equipment, but this does not affect the lighting of the control panel.

(2)   STDBY: All power supplies are switched ON, but the receiver is rendered inoperative.

(3)   LOW: The receiver is ON but is sensitive only to strong interroga- tion signals from nearby stations.

(4)   NORM: The receiver is at maximum sensitivity and the equipment responds to interrogation from distant stations.

(5)   EMERGENCY: The receiver is at maximum sensitivity and the equipment responds to interrogation in any mode with the emergency reply.

NOTE

To select EMERGENCY, spring loaded button adjacent to the rotary selector must be depressed. This button prevents accidental selection of the emergency operation.

(b)   MODE 2 switch: Is a two position switch controlling operation of the equipment on Mode 2, with switch positions as follows:

(1)   OUT: The equipment will respond to normal Mode 1 interrogations. It will not respond to Mode 2 except to transmit the emergency response if the master switch is selected to EMERGENCY.

(2)   MODE 2: The equipment will respond to MODE 1 and MODE 2 interrogations.

(c)   MODE 3 switch: Is a two position switch for controlling Mode 3 operation, with switch positions as follows:

(1)   OUT: The equipment will respond to Mode 1 interrogations. It will not respond to MODE 3 except to transmit the emergency response if the master switch is set to EMERGENCY.

(2)   MODE 3: The equipment will respond to MODE 1 and MODE 3 interrogations.

(d)   I/P-OUT-MIC switch is a three position switch for special operation of the system on Mode 2, with switch positions as follows:

(1)   I/P: Switch position is inoperative.

(2)   OUT: Will respond to interrogations normally.

(3)   MIC: Will respond to Mode 2 interrogations whenever the UHF transmitter is energized.

214.   For automatic operation of the IFF upon seat ejection, see para 240.

215.   The IFF system shares two antennas with the TACAN system (if the TACAN system is fitted). They are the upper and lower "L" band antennas. A two position "L" band antenna transfer switch is mounted on the navigator's RH console, marked IFF UP/TACAN LOW and IFF LOW/TACAN UP. The switch allows the antennas to be connected to the systems as selected.

EJECTION SEATS

General

216.   The pilot and navigator are each provided with a MK C5 automatic ejection seat to enable them to abandon the aircraft. Ejection from ground level at aircraft speeds as low as 80 knots IAS, is made possible by the high ejection velocity and the rapid deployment of the parachute.

217.   The ejection seats are made safe when the aircraft is at rest by installing safety pins at the following locations:

(a)   The seat firing gear and the canopy cartridge firing mechanism sear. These two safety pins are attached to a common chain with a warning plate. Alternatively, the canopy sear pin of this assembly may be used to lock the overhead firing handle. In this case, the seat firing sear pin is not used.

(b)   The drogue gun safety lock.

(c)   The alternative firing handle.

Interconnected Firing System of the Canopy and Ejection Seat

218.   The emergency opening of the canopy and ejection of the seat is achieved by means of cartridges. The canopy is forced open by a single cartridge, while the seat is fired by an ejection gun containing a primary and two secondary cartridges.

219.   The canopy cartridge and ejection gun cartridge are fired by pulling a large horizontal firing handle fitted immediately above the headrest. The firing handle is attached to a canvas face blind which is pulled over the occupant's face. Alternatively, the canopy and ejection gun can be fired by pulling upwards on the alternative firing handle located on the seat pan between the occupant's knees. This firing handle is for use should the seat occupant find it impossible to reach or operate the overhead firing handle.

220.   The operation of either of these firing handles withdraws two sears, one sear for the canopy cartridge firing mechanism and one sear for the ejection gun. The cartridge of the canopy firing mechanism is detonated immediately but the firing of the ejection gun does not take place until the canopy is in its emergency open position.

221.   When the canopy cartridge is fired the gas generated unlocks the canopy latches and, through uncovered ports, passes to the actuating mechanism jack. Through linkage, the canopy is forced open and is retained open by a spring-loaded hook.

222.   During the canopy opening process the firing pin of the ejection gun is prevented from moving by a release rod, but as soon as the canopy passes its normal open position the release rod begins to withdraw from the firing pin. When the canopy has opened sufficiently to give clearance for the path of the seat, the release rod is fully withdrawn and allows the spring-loaded firing pin to detonate the primary cartridge of the ejection gun. The firing of the secondary cartridges is then caused by flame from the primary cartridge.

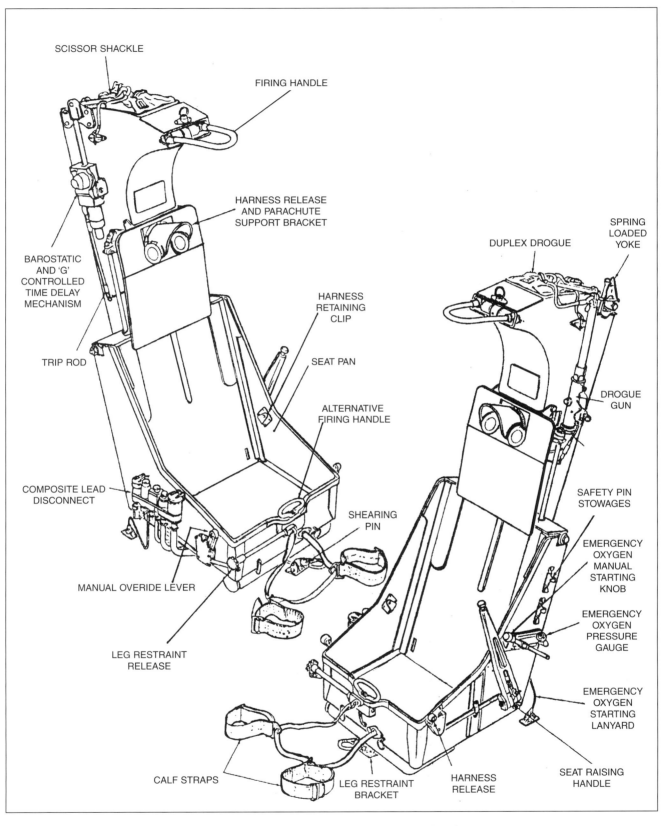

FIG-1-6 MK C5 EJECTION SEAT

223.   As the seat leaves the aircraft, the occupant's legs are pulled to the rear and held against the front of the seat pan by means of a leg restraint cord. They are held in this position until separation from the seat takes place. Movement of the seat also breaks the quick disconnect between the seat and the aircraft, primes the drogue gun and the time release mechanism by removing their respective sears, and operates the emergency oxygen bottle by means of a lanyard.

224.   Approximately one-half second after the seat and occupant have been ejected the cartridge operated drogue gun withdraws a controller drogue from a container behind the headrest. This drogue tilts the seat into a horizontal attitude and then withdraws the main 5 foot drogue from the container. The main drogue further decelerates and steadies the seat.

225.   A barostatic and 'g' controlled time-delay mechanism is fitted to the top of the RH side beam. Provided ejection takes place below 5000 metres (16,400 feet), and that the forward deceleration of the seat is less than 4 g, the time-delay mechanism will operate after 1.3 seconds. If ejection occurs at a higher altitude, a barostat attached to the time-release mechanism prevents the release from functioning until the seat and occupant have fallen to 5000 metres (16,400 feet). The barostat in the first aircraft is set to 10,000 feet.

226.   When the time-delay mechanism operates it releases the parachute harness from its attachments to the seat at three points and disconnects the seat portion from the crew member portion of the composite leads disconnect. It also releases the leg restraining cords and the drogue line from the seat. The drogue line now pulls on a lifting line which extracts the parachute pack pin and withdraws the main parachute from the pack. The seat is allowed to fall free.

Manual Override Control

227.   Provision is made to manually disconnect the parachute withdrawal line from the parachute static line by means of the parachute override 'D' ring. A separate lever control is fitted to manually release the parachute and parachute harness from the seat. These manually operated controls enable the seat occupant to separate himself from the seat should the seat fail to eject or, after ejection, if the automatic separation mechanism fails to function.

228.   The override 'D' ring is a conventional ring partly covered by a small flap secured by press-studs. When the flap is removed and the override 'D' ring is pulled, the parachute withdrawal line is disconnected from the parachute static line. This action also uncovers the inner rip-cord 'D' ring. The manual override lever is fitted on the RH side of the seat pan and is normally locked in the fully forward position by a spring catch under the head of the lever engaging in a slot of the lever quadrant. Releasing the spring catch and moving the lever fully to the rear until the catch engages in the rear slot of the quadrant will perform the following operations automatically:

(a)   Release the parachute and parachute harness from the seat.

(b)   Release the leg restraint cords from the seat.

(c)   Release the crew member portion of the composite leads disconnect from the seat portion.

Manual Leg Restraint Release

229.   A small handwheel is fitted at the front of the RH side of the seat pan. Turning the handwheel will operate the release on the front of the seat pan and free the leg restraint cords from the seat.

Harness Release

230.   A lever is fitted on the forward LH side of the seat pan. Movement of the lever to the rear allows the seat occupant to lean forward against the pull of a spring-loaded harness reel. As the occupant leans back the harness will be snubbed at all positions and the lever must be operated to lean forward again.

Seat Raising Handle

231.   A lever is fitted on the LH side of the seat. By depressing a spring-loaded plunger in the end of the lever, and moving the lever up or down, the seat pan will raise or lower. When the plunger is released it will engage in one of several locating holes and lock the seat pan in position.

232.   Further information on the ejection seat is contained in Arrow I Service Data - Section 31 - Ejection Seat, Mk C5.

EMERGENCY EQUIPMENT

Engine Fire Detection and Extinguishing System

233.   A system of cable type fire detectors are located in three potential fire areas. These areas are the RH engine compartment, the LH engine compartment and the hydraulic and equipment bay. The detectors sense a fire or an overheat condition existing in these areas and cause the illumination of warning lights. Two container bottles of fire extinguishing chemical are carried. For the first flights three additional bottles are fitted in the armament bay. These are operated by the existing switches.

234.   The fire warning and extinguishing panel marked FIRE is mounted on the LH console in the pilot's cockpit. The panel contains three red lights marked LH, HYD, RH; the lights are provided with transparent covers. A toggle switch protected by a guard is marked SECOND SHOT. A second toggle switch protected by a guard is marked CRASH FIRE.

235.   Fire indication is given by the illumination of the master red warning light on the main instrument panel. At the same time a red warning light will illuminate on the FIRE warning/ extinguishing panel. The particular light that illuminates will indicate the location of the fire.

236.   The extinguisher is operated by lifting the cover and pressing the illuminated bulb on the FIRE panel. This action will release one bottle of extinguishing chemical into the appropriate fire area. The remaining bottle of extinguishing chemical may be discharged into the same fire area if the warning light does not go out, by lifting the cover and selecting the SECOND SHOT switch.

Alternatively, should a fire occur in either of the other two areas, the second bottle may be used by pressing the appropriate warning light. (On the first aircraft operating either engine fire extinguisher will discharge two bottles into the affected area. Operating the HYD bay extinguisher will discharge one bottle into that bay.)

CAUTION

Should a fire occur in either the LH or RH engine compartments, the appropriate HP and LP fuel cocks should be selected off before operating the fire extinguisher. (See part 3 of para 15.)

237.   The CRASH FIRE switch distributes the contents of the fire extinguisher bottles in the event of a crash landing. The switch should be operated after the throttles have been placed in the "cut-off" position and the LP FUEL COCKS have been switched off. Operating the switch will discharge the contents of one bottle into the hydraulic and equipment bay and the contents of the other bottle will be divided between the LH and RH engine bays. (On the first aircraft, when the three additional bottles are fitted, the crash switch will discharge two bottles into the hydraulic and equipment bay and one and one-half bottles into each engine bay).

238.   Power for the fire extinguishing system is taken from the emergency bus and therefore the system will operate regardless of the position of the master electrical switch.

Bail-out Signal

239.   A switch, protected by a guard and marked NAV BAIL OUT is located on the LH console, aft of the power controls. Operating the switch will illuminate a red warning light on the navigator's panel marked BAIL OUT and a signal horn will be energized to warn the navigator to eject. A green light on the pilot's main instrument panel, marked NAV BAIL OUT, will also illuminate. The green light will go out when the navigator ejects. Power is supplied from the emergency bus.

Emergency Operation of the UHF and IFF on Seat Ejection

240.   Upon the ejection of either seat from the aircraft, a switch located on the seat bulkhead is actuated and causes emergency operation of the IFF. At the same time the emergency channel of the UHF set is energized and causes an MCW signal to be transmitted. Provided the IFF and UHF had previously been selected on, the signals transmitted will enable ground stations to obtain a fix on the aircraft's position.

241.   A test push button switch marked PRESS-TO-TEST - UHF/IFF EMERG is located on the pilot's RH console. Testing should be carried out according to Telecommunication Confidential Orders.

Parabrake

242.   A brake parachute is fitted in the rear end of the fuselage and is mechanically controlled through cables by a lever which has STREAM and JETTISON positions. The lever is located in the pilot's cockpit, aft of the engine power controls. The parachute is released through two doors above the stinger by moving the lever downwards to the STREAM position. The action of the parachute when released slows the aircraft after landing. A shear pin is fitted which will shear if the parachute is released during flight. The parachute may be jettisoned after completing the landing run, or in an emergency, by moving the control lever inwards and downwards to the JETTISON position. An indicator is fitted below the tail cone and is visible when a parachute is not installed. The installation of a parachute raises the indicator flush with the skin.

FLIGHT INSTRUMENTS

Pitot-Static System

243.   Three pressure heads are fitted to the aircraft and supply pitot and static air pressure to the various instruments, controllers and transducers. One pressure head is installed on the forward end of the air data probe at the aircraft nose, while two are fitted to the leading edge of the fin. The lower pressure head on the fin is used for flight test instrumentation only, while the upper is utilized by the flying control emergency damping system transducer.

244.   The pitot and static pressure from the nose pressure head is transmitted to the Mach/airspeed indicator and the flying control normal damping system transducer. The static pressure, in addition, serves the altimeters, rate of climb indicator, cabin pressure regulator and safety pressure valve controllers.

Mach/Airspeed Indicator

245.   The Mach/Airspeed Indicator is mounted on the pilot's main instrument panel. Indicated airspeed and mach number are displayed on a single dial, and a striped pointer provides a constant indication of the maximum allowable airspeed at any altitude. An adjustable index allows a landing speed to be pre-set. The split airspeed pointer indicates mach number on the inner scale, with the corresponding IAS on the outer scale.

Altimeter

246.   An altimeter is mounted on the main instrument panel in both cockpits. The instrument has three pointers and incorporates a cut-out window. The largest pointer registers hundreds of feet, the intermediate pointer registers thousands of feet while the small pointer indicates tens of thousands of feet. A striped area is progressively covered during a climb and is uncovered again upon descending. During descent, the striped area commences to uncover at 16,700 feet, and is fully uncovered at zero feet. This warning provides an additional indication, during a rapid descent, that the aircraft is approaching the lower altitudes.

Skin Temperature Indicator

247.   A skin temperature indicator is mounted on the LH side of the pilot's main instrument panel. During flight the instrument registers the temperature of the aircraft skin taken from the underside of the radar nose. When the aircraft is on the ground the indicator registers the outside air temperature.

Sideslip and Angle of Attack Indicators

248.   A sideslip indicator and an angle of attack indicator are mounted on the pilot's main instrument panel. Vanes, fitted to the air data probe, sense any change in direction of the relative airflow to the aircraft datum, both in the lateral and vertical axes. Movement of the vanes is transmitted to the indicators and the angle of sideslip and/or the angle of attack of the aircraft are shown on the appropriate indicators in degrees.

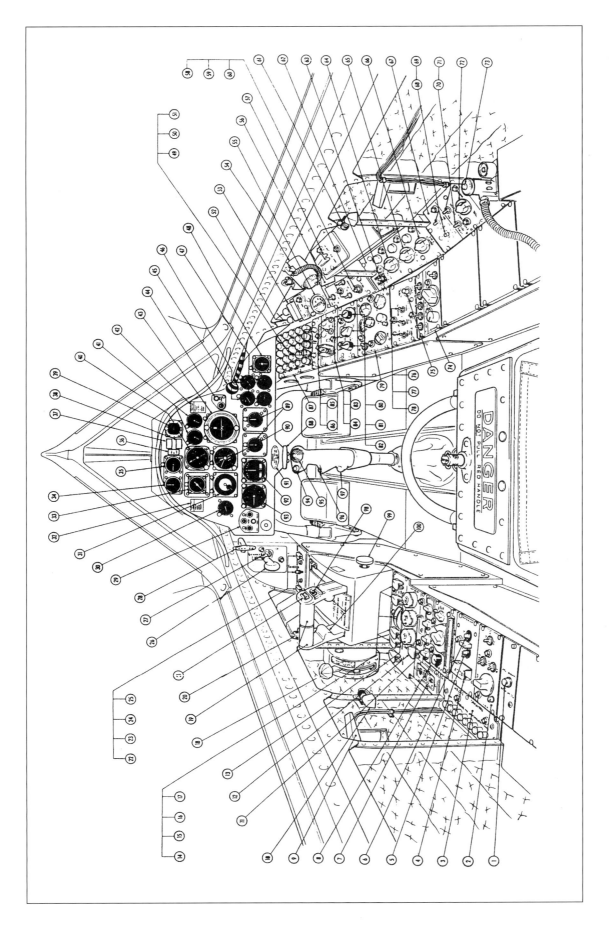

FIG-1-7 PILOT'S COCKPIT LAYOUT

1 U/C UP MODE - DAMPER TEST
2 IFF Control Panel
3 DAMPING SYSTEM Circuit Breaker Panel
4 DAMPER, POWER ON-OFF Switch
5 DAMPER, EMERGENCY Push Button Switch
6 DAMPER, ENGAGE Push Button Switch
7 Control Surface Response Indicator
8 COMM, Radio Control Panel - ARC-34
9 High Altitude Flood Light
10 Console Flood Light
11 RUDDER TRIM, LEFT-RIGHT Switch
12 FIRE Extinguisher, SECOND SHOT Switch
13 FIRE-Combined Warning Lights and Selector Switches, LH, HYD, RH
14 NAV BAIL OUT Warning Switch
15 L.P. FUEL COCKS Switches and Guards
16 CROSSFEED, LH ONLY - NORMAL - RH ONLY Switch
17 ENGINE FUEL, EMERG-RESET Switches and Guards
18 Parachute Brake, STREAM - JETTISON Selector Lever
19 Throttle Levers, LH and RH
20 Console Flood Light
21 SPEED BRAKE, IN-OUT Switch
22 ANTI-SKID, NORM-EMERG-OFF Switch
23 LIGHTS LAND-TAXI-OFF Switch
24 CANOPY CLOSE-OFF-OPEN Switch
25 ELEV TRIM DISENGAGE Switch
26 Landing Gear Control Lever, UP-DN
27 Landing Gear EMERGENCY EXTENSION Locking Latch Push-Button
28 Parking Brake Handle
29 LANDING GEAR POSITION Indicator
30 SKIN TEMP Indicator
31 Mach/Airspeed Indicator
32 CHECK LIST, LANDING

33 Accelerometer
34 Sideslip Indicator
35 Angle of Attack Indicator
36 NAV BAIL OUT Indicator
37 Red Master Warning Light
38 Amber Master Warning Light
39 Standby Magnetic Compass
40 RADIO MAGNETIC INDICATOR
41 FUEL QUANTITY Gauges
42 CHECK LIST TAKE OFF
43 Artificial Horizon Indicator
44 GYRO ERECT Push Button
45 EMERGENCY CANOPY OPENING Lever
46 Engine PRESSURE RATIO Gauges LH and RH
47 EXH TEMP Gauges LH and RH
48 CABIN PRESSURE ALTITUDE Gauge
49 PRESS TO RESET Push Button
50 DAY - NIGHT Switch
51 PRESS TO TEST Switch
52 ENG BLEED Air Conditioning Warning Lights
53 ENG BLEED AIR LH OFF-NORMAL-RH OFF Switch
54 Map Light
55 OXYGEN Quantity Guage
56 Console Flood Lights (2)
57 RAM AIR TURBINE Switch
58 NAV LIGHTS, FLASH-OFF-STEADY Switch
59 ALTERNATORS RESET ON-OFF LH and RH Switches
60 DC RESET Push Button
61 Console Light
62 COCKPIT LIGHTING Panel
63 HIGH ALT LIGHTING ON-OFF Switch
64 MAIN PANEL OFF-BRIGHT Selector
65 CONSOLE PANELS OFF-BRIGHT Selector
66 CONSOLE FLOOD OFF-BRIGHT Selector
67 AIR COND Panel

68 RAIN REPELLENT ON-OFF Switch (TEMP CONTROL/EMERG OFF: First aircraft)
69 CABIN PRESS DUMP Switch
70 AIR SUPPLY NORM-OFF EMERG Switch
71 DEFOG ON-OFF Switch
72 TEMP COOL-WARM Selector
73 Anti-g Valve Manual Override Button
74 INTER Control Panel
75 UHF/IFF EMERG, PRESS TO TEST Button
76 J4 COMP, AEROBATICS - NORMAL Switch
77 UHF ANT, UPPER-LOWER Switch
78 RMI NEEDLE, TACAN-UHF HOMER Switch
79 RADIO COMPASS Panel
80 J4 COMP - LAT Correction Controller
81 J4 COMP - NAG/DG Selector Switch
82 J4 COMP - DECR/INCR/SET Switch
83 J4 COMP - Hemisphere Selector Switch
84 J4 COMP - Synchronizing Indicator (Annunciator)
85 ENGINE START, START-OFF-RESET, LH an RH Switches
86 MASTER ELEC ON-OFF Switch
87 Warning Lights Panel
88 Rudder PEDAL ADJUST Handle
89 RPM Indicators
90 Altimeter
91 Rudder Pedal Adjustment Label
92 Turn and Slip Indicator
93 Rate of Climb Indicator
94 Automatic Mode Disengage Switch
95 Elevator and Aileron Trim Button
96 Emergency Damping Engage Switch
97 Nose Wheel Steering Selector
98 Press-to-transmit Push Button
99 Throttle Friction Damper
100 Engine Relight Switch, LH and RH

PILOT'S COCKPIT LAYOUT

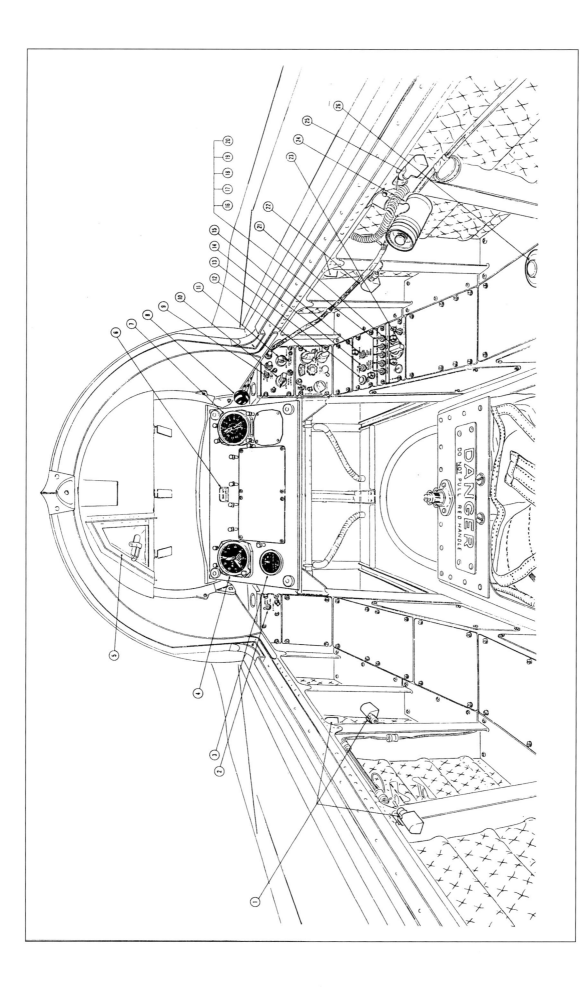

FIG 1-8 NAVIGATOR'S COCKPIT LAYOUT

NAVIGATOR'S COCKPIT

1. Console Flood Lights (3)
2. CANOPY, OPEN-OFF-CLOSE Switch
3. OXYGEN Quantity Gauge
4. Altimeter
5. Access Panel to Navigator's Canopy Locking Handle from Front Cockpit
6. Navigator's BAILOUT Warning Light
7. RADIO MAGNETIC INDICATOR
8. EMERGENCY CANOPY OPENING Lever
9. HIGH ALT LIGHTING, ON-OFF Switch (Non-operative)
10. PANEL LIGHTS OFF-BRIGHT Selector Switch
11. CONSOLE FLOOD OFF-BRIGHT Selector Switch
12. RADIO COMPASS Control Panel ARN-6
13. PRESS TO TALK Switch
14. IFF-TACAN ANTENNA SELECT Switch
15. UHF HOMER - TACAN RMI NEEDLE Selector
16. INTER, Interphone Mixing Switch
17. COMP, Radio Compass Mixing Switch
18. COMM, Command Receiver Mixing Switch
19. TACAN Mixing Switch
20. TEL, Telescramble Mixing Switch
21. INTER Control Panel AIC-10
22. Console Flood Lights (2)
23. CALL, INTER, COMM, TEL Rotary Selector
24. Map and Emergency Light
25. Console Flood Light
26. Anti-g Suit Pressure Regulator Manual Override

PART 2

HANDLING

PRELIMINARIES

Before Entering the Aircraft

1.   Check RCAF Form L14A for fuel, oil and oxygen quantities, and signatures completed throughout by tradesmen concerned. Note unserviceabilities, if any.

2.   Compute engine pressure ratio for take-off.

3.   Carry out the Exterior Inspection as shown on Fig. 2-1.

Solo Flying

4.   If the aircraft is to be flown with the rear cockpit unoccupied, check in the rear cockpit:

(a)   Harness secured.

(b)   All loose articles of equipment removed and stowed.

(c)   Safety pins in position in seat sear, canopy sear, drogue gun and alternate firing handle.

(d)   Rear canopy locked.

Before Entering the Cockpits

5.   Make the following checks (front and rear seat occupants as applicable):

(a)   Check the emergency oxygen pressure gauge; a fully charged cylinder registers 1800 psi.

(b)   Check that the drogue gun static lines are attached to the bracket on the ejection gun body.

After Entering the Cockpit

6.   Make the following checks. (Front and rear seat occupants as applicable):

(a)   Check that the ejection seat manual override control lever is locked fully forward.

(b)   Fasten and adjust the parachute/safety harness and the leg restraint straps.

(c)   Adjust the seat height in order to position the head correctly in relation to the headrest and adjust the rudder pedals for reach. Check the rudder pedals for correct adjustment.

(d)   Plug in the radio, oxygen and anti-g suit connections to the composite leads disconnect fitting.

(e)   Check that the ground crew remove and stow the safety pins from the sears of the ejection gun, drogue gun and the canopy. The alternative firing handle safety pin can only be removed by the seat occupant, and it should be stowed by the ground crew.

(f)   Check that all individual electrical switches are OFF.

NOTE

The ALTERNATOR switches, LP COCK and DAMPER POWER switches may normally be left on.

(g)   Check that the U/C selector lever is down, and that the position of the speed brakes selector corresponds to the speed brakes position before energizing the electrical system.

(h)   Signal the ground crew to plug the ground starter cart and the external AC power supply into the aircraft receptacles.

(j)   Switch the Master Electrics switch - ON.

NOTE

When the Master Electrics switch is switched on the FUEL PROP and FUEL LOW warning lights may illuminate momentarily.

(k)   Check that the AC FAIL and DC FAIL warning lights are out. On the first flights of the first aircraft the BATT USE light will remain on until an engine is started. The battery is not isolated when the DC supply is plugged in.

(m)   AIC-10 switches (as required).
                INTER mixing switch ON.
                COMM mixing switch ON.
                Rotary selector - COMM.

(n)   ARC-34 transmitter-receiver (as required).
                Function selector switch - BOTH.
                Operational mode push selector - PRESET.
                Frequency selector switch to the desired channel.

(p)   J4 COMPASS (as required).
                MAG - DG switch to MAG.
                NORMAL/AEROBATICS switch to NORMAL.

(q)   IFF selector switch to STANDBY.

(r)   Air conditioning -
                AIR SUPPLY switch to NORM.
                CABIN PRESS/DUMP switch to CABIN PRESS.
                DEFOG switch - as required.
                Cabin TEMP-COOL/WARM rheostat switch mid position.
                TEMP CONTROL switch - normal position (Upright).

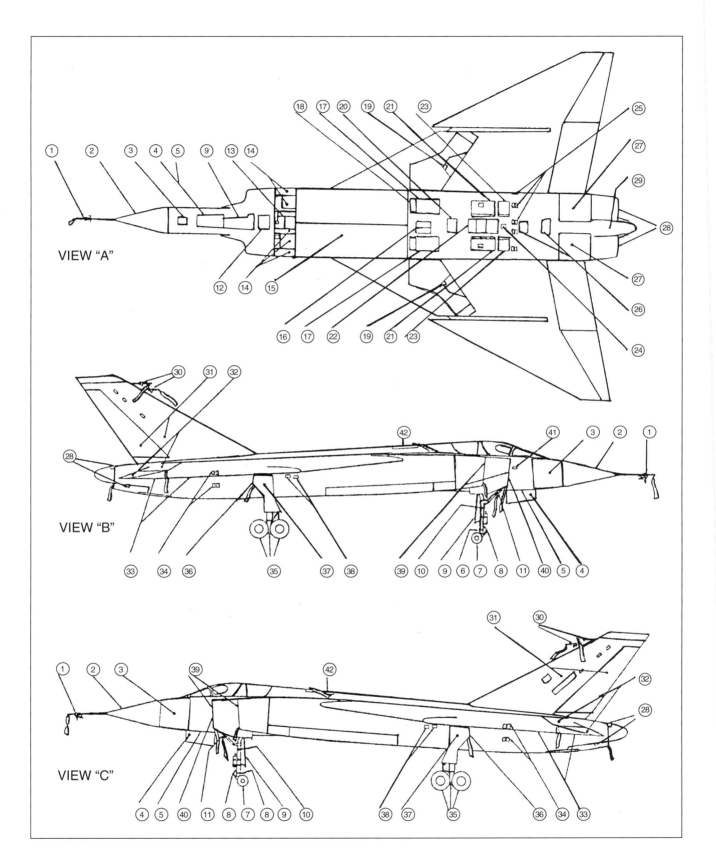

VIEW "A"

VIEW "B"

VIEW "C"

FIG 2-1 EXTERIOR INSPECTION

Nose (View A-B-C)

(1)   Probe secure and cover removed.

(2)   Radome secure.

(3)   Radar access doors (three) secure.

(4)   Nose U/C door undamaged.

(5)   Nose wheel well.
        a) Emergency nitrogen bottle pressure - 5000 psi minimum.
        (b) Circuit breakers set.

(6)   Landing and taxi lights undamaged.

(7)   Tires for cuts and creep, nose wheel aligned fore and aft.

(8)   Shock absorber strut extension normal.

(9)   Condition of nose U/C leg door.

(10)   No hydraulic leaks.

(11)   Nose wheel ground locking pin removed.

Underside of Aircraft (View A)

(12)   Air conditioning equipment access panel secure.

(13)   (a) Electronic equipment access door secure.
        (b) Circuit breakers set (visual through inspection port).

(14)   LH and RH electronic equipment access doors secure.

(15)   Instrument pack for damage. Check for security.

(16)   Electrical equipment access doors secure.

(17)   LH and RH speed brakes for damage.

(18)   Master refuelling/test panel door. closed.

(19)   Pressure refuelling LH and RH access doors secured. (On the first aircraft check the manually operated gate valves are set to FLIGHT POSITION VALVE OPEN.)

(20)   Hydraulic equipment access panel secure.

(21)   LH and RH engine access doors secured.

(22)   Service panel No. 1, gearbox panel and service panel No. 2 secured.

(23)   Engine access doors secured.

(24)   Compensator removal panel secure.

(25)   "Blow-in" air inlet doors closed.

(26)   Service panels No. 3 and No. 4 secure.

(27)   LH and RH engine removal doors secure.

Rear of Aircraft (View A-B-C)

(28)   Jet pipe exhaust covers removed. Jet pipes undamaged. Check for fuel, oil, water or ice accumulation.

(29)   (a) Parabrake doors closed.
        (b) Red indicator NOT protruding. (Denoting 'chute' installed).

LH Side of Aircraft (View C)

(30)   Pitot covers removed.

(31)   Fin and rudder surfaces, navigation lights, access panels for security and damage.

(32)   Aileron and elevators for damage and control support removed.

(33)   Underside of skin for fuel leaks or damage. Leading edge undamaged.

(34)   "Blow-in" air inlet doors closed.

(35)   (a) Check for red crank pointer touching recuperator body. (Nitrogen pressure indicator).
        (b) Check recuperator oil level.
        (c) Leg extension normal.
        (d) Tires for cuts and creep.
        (e) No hydraulic leaks.

(36)   Main wheel ground lock on side stay removed.

(37)   (a) U/C fairings undamaged.
        (b) Check lower spring housing locking cams on fairings.

(38)   Access doors secure.

(39)   (a) LH Engine intake cover removed.
        (b) De-icing boots on intake and ramp undamaged.

(40)   Air conditioning ram air inlet cover removed.

RH Side of Aircraft (View B)

Check as for LH side, items 31 to 40.

(41)   Emergency canopy opening panel secure.

Upper Surfaces of Aircraft

Visually inspect the upper surfaces (including windscreen and canopies) for damage and security of panels prior to entering the cockpit.

(42)   Ensure that the air conditioning outlet duct cover is removed.

NOTE

With the external air supply plugged into the aircraft, the above air conditioning switches will be inoperative. However, selections made at this time will be operative when the external air supply is disconnected, and full air supply will be available when the landing gear is raised after take-off.

(s)   Operate the PRESS-TO-TEST switch on the warning light panel and check that the warning lights illuminate. Release the switch and check that the lights go out. OIL PRESS and ENG FUEL PRESS warning lights will remain on, and the hydraulic pressure warning lights may remain on.

(t)   Landing and taxi lights - check operation. Switch OFF. (Landing and taxi lights are not fitted for the first flights of the first aircraft.)

(u)   Landing Gear - Lever in the DOWN position, warning light in handle not illuminated, and gear indicator showing landing gear locked down.

(v)   Fuel Contents - Registered correctly.

(w)   Check ENGINE FUEL switch at NORMAL.

(y)   Check A.S.I. limiting speed pointer is set.

(z)   Operate the NAV BAIL OUT switch. Check that the NAV BAIL OUT green light in the front cockpit illuminates. Check with the navigator that the red BAIL OUT light illuminates and that the warning buzzer sounds. Return the switch to off.

(aa)   Throttle levers in the cut-off position.

(ab)   DAMPER POWER switch - check ON.

(ac)   Artificial horizon erected. If necessary press gyro ERECTION button after gyro has run up for 30 seconds. OFF indicator not visible.

(ad)   Turn and bank indicator erected. OFF indicator not visible.

(ae)   Check oxygen mask for fit and test for flow. Check quantity.

(af)   Front and rear cockpit canopies closed and fully locked.

CAUTION

Check that the canopy lever is in the extreme forward position and not in the detent position. In the detent position the canopy will lock, but the seals will not inflate, and the lever will not be free of the latch mechanism. The lever is nearly horizontal when locked fully forward.

STARTING PROCEDURE

Preliminaries

7.   If starting one engine at a time, always start the RH engine first to check functioning of the RH pumps on the flying control and utility systems. The LH pumps may be checked on engine shut down by stopping the RH engine first.

WARNING

All personnel must be kept clear of both intake and jet pipe.
(See Fig. 2-2 JET WAKE diagram in colour section page 21).

Procedure for starting

8.   Adopt the following sequence:

(a)   Check with ground crew as follows:

    (1)   Intercom functions satisfactorily.

    (2)   Cockpit access stand clear of aircraft.

    (3)   Fire extinguisher in position.

(b)   Parking brake ON.

(c)   Check that the master electrical switch is ON.

(d)   Throttles - Cut-off position.

(e)   Check fuel:

    (1)   CROSSFEED - NORMAL

    (2)   LP cocks ON.

(f)   On receipt of the "ready to start signal" from the ground engine start operator, advance the appropriate throttle lever to the IDLE position and immediately pulse the appropriate ENGINE START switch to START.

(g)   Check turbine outlet temperature. A temperature rise within 10-15 seconds indicates engine "light-up". On the first aircraft the turbine outlet temperature gauge is operated by external AC supply, which must be plugged in to obtain a reading. On later aircraft the gauge will be supplied with AC power from the starter cart.

NOTE

The engine will accelerate to approximately 55% rpm. Turbine outlet temperature should not exceed 600°C, except momentarily, during the transition period to idle rpm. At idle rpm the turbine outlet temperature should drop to 340°C or below.

(h)   Check OIL PRESS and FUEL PRESS warning lights out. Check hydraulic pressure warning lights out, if they were illuminated before starting.

(j)   Check ENGINE EMERG FUEL light out.

(k)   Repeat the starting procedure for the other engine.

(m)   Check that the ALTERNATOR switches are on.

NOTE

When the AC ground power supply is disconnected, the aircraft alternators will automatically take over. Upon disconnection, check that the AC FAIL and DC FAIL warning lights remain out.

CAUTION

If the engines have been cold-soaked to a temperature of −35°C or below, allow the engines to idle for five minutes in order to warm up.

Engine at Idle

9.   Check with the ground crew by means of the intercom that the engine overboard bleed valve is in the "open" position, that the air ejector nozzle is operating (indicated by visual overboard discharge) and that the spring loaded air inlet doors to the engine bay are in the "open" position.

Wet Start

10.   If, during the normal starting sequence, no rise in temperature is observed within 20 seconds of opening the throttle lever to the idle position, a wet start has occurred and the following procedure should be carried out:

(a)   Bring the throttle lever back to the cut-off position.

(b)   Hold the engine start switch to RESET for a period of 30 seconds only, then release the switch and carry out the normal starting procedure.

(c)   Should another wet start occur, bring the throttle lever back to cut-off position.

(d)   Switch the master electrics switch OFF.

(e)   Investigate the cause of failure to light up.

Hot Start

11.   If, during the normal starting sequence, the turbine discharge temperature rises above 600°C for more than five seconds, the engine must be stopped immediately by placing the throttle to cut-off. The engine start switch should be selected to RESET momentarily; this will break the ignition circuit and shut off the ground starter air supply. Investigate the cause of the hot start before attempting a relight.

NOTE

All hot starts where a temperature of 600°C is exceeded must be recorded on Form L14A.

CAUTION

A maximum of three starting runs in 10 minutes is permissible. Two of these runs may be of 30 seconds duration and run consecutively.

FLYING CONTROLS CHECK (To be issued later.)

TAXIING PROCEDURE

General

12.   When the chocks have been removed and the brakes released, only a very small increase in engine power is necessary to start the aircraft moving. When taxiing, idle thrust is sufficient to keep the aircraft moving at a speed of approximately 25-50 mph.

Nose Wheel Steering

13.   Nose wheel steering is engaged by aligning the rudder pedals to the corresponding nose wheel position and depressing the nose wheel steering push button located at the bottom left of the control column hand grip. The button must be maintained depressed during steering operations. The aircraft is steered by slowing moving the rudder pedals in the required turn direction.

NOTE

Movement of the nose wheel is governed to a maximum turning rate of 19° per second. Rapid movement of the rudder pedals or increased pressure on them will not affect the rate of turn of the nose wheel.

14.   Steering is disengaged by releasing the button on the control column, when normal castoring action of the nose wheel is restored.

CAUTION

Use of brakes when nose wheel steering is in operation is still under investigation. If brakes are used at all, they must be applied carefully and at low speed only.

TAKE-OFF PROCEDURE   )

ACTIONS AFTER TAKE-OFF) (To be issued later.)

FLYING CHARACTERISTICS)

LANDING PROCEDURE   )

ENGINE HANDLING

Engine Pressure Ratio During Afterburning

15.   When the afterburners are turned on, the engine pressure ratio may increase or decrease slightly. The acceptable variation will be published when available.

Low Pressure Compressor Overspeed Warning Light

16.   When the afterburners are turned on, the LH and RH ROTOR O'SPEED lights may illuminate momentarily. This condition is normal and serves as an indication that the compressor overspeed light and mechanism are functioning normally.

Engine Fuel System Failure

17.   When operating on the EMERG fuel system, do not return the ENGINE FUEL switch to NORMAL for the remainder of the flight. This may result in engine flame-out. If checking the system in the air, the transfer back to NORMAL must be carried out with the power lever at idle to avoid a pressure surge in the fuel system.

18.   The procedure for returning the fuel system to NORMAL, after ground checks or in the air is as follows:
(a)   Power lever of affected engine to IDLE.

(b)   Select ENGINE FUEL switch to RESET and hold for approximately 3 to 5 seconds after the EMERG FUEL warning light goes out.

(c)   Allow the switch to return to NORMAL.

Thrust Overshoot

19.   When using engine pressure ratio to check engine power prior to take-off, a thrust overshoot may be noted when the power lever is advanced from idle to military thrust on a cold engine. This thrust overshoot will gradually diminish to the specified or computer value within five minutes or less. The condition is considered to be normal; however, it must not be relied upon for added performance during take-off.

END OF FLIGHT PROCEDURE

Stopping the Engines

20.   Whenever the engines have been operated at high power settings for an appreciable length of time, they must be allowed to idle for up to five minutes prior to shutdown.

21.   Stop the RH engine first by moving the RH power lever to the cut-off position. Operate the flying controls and check that the utility hydraulics and the flying control hydraulic warning lights do not illuminate. Stop the LH engine by moving the LH power lever to the cut-off position.

Action Before Leaving the Aircraft

22.   Proceed as follows:

PART 2

(a)   Master electrics switch OFF.

(b)   Centralize the control column and rudder pedals.

(c)   Parking brake ON.

23.   With the flying controls in neutral, the control surfaces will be streamlined and locked against adverse wind forces. However, in a short time, full aileron and elevator "droop" will occur. If the aircraft is to be on the ground for any length of time, the hydraulic system pressure should be dissipated. Hold the control column central and move the rudder pedals slightly until no further movement of the rudder surface takes place. When this operation has been performed, the ground crew must fit the special aileron and elevator supports to the control surfaces to support their weight and prevent strain on the control linkages.

PART 3

EMERGENCY HANDLING

ENGINE FAILURE PROCEDURE

Engine Failure During Take-off - To be issued later.

One Engine Failure in Flight

1.   If an engine fails in flight proceed as follows:

(a)   Immediately close the throttle to idle and attempt to relight the engine.

(b)   If the engine will not relight after one attempt, proceed as follows:

      (1)   Close the relevant throttle to cut-off position.

      (2)   Follow the relight procedure in para 5.

(c)   If relight is inadvisable, adjust the trim for asymmetric flight.

(d)   Select fuel crossfeed as required to balance fuel load.

Two-Engine Failure in Flight

2.   If fuel is still available and the aircraft has sufficient altitude, and if there are no apparent mechanical defects in the engines, proceed as follows:

(a)   (1)   Maintain airspeed above 250 knots EAS to provide pressure for the flying control hydraulics.

      OR, (if the ram air turbine is fitted)

      (2)   If the speed is below 350 knots EAS select RAM AIR TURBINE switch ON.

(b)   Carry out the relight procedure for one engine. If unsuccessful attempt to relight the other engine (See para 4 and 5).

NOTE

Do not use speed brakes unless absolutely necessary as they require pressure from the utility hydraulic system. This system is, in the above emergency, driving the emergency alternator.

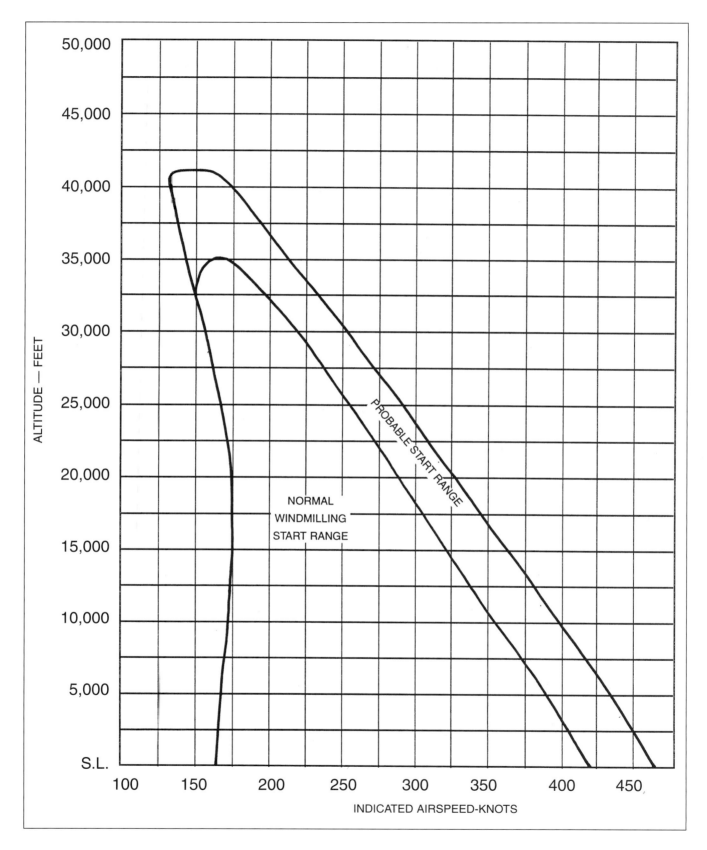

FIG 3-1 J75 RELIGHT CHART

EMERGENCY RELIGHT IN THE AIR

General

3.   The J-75 engine will relight at any combination of airspeed and altitude which falls within the "Normal Windmilling Start Range" indicated on Fig. 3-1. The "Probable Start Range" represents those combinations of airspeed and altitude at which engine relights may frequently, but not always, be made. For best results, when operating above the maximum altitude and airspeed combinations indicated in the "Normal Windmilling Start Range," reduce either the airspeed, the altitude or both until they are within the ranges shown on the chart.

Relight Procedure

4.   Relights may sometimes be obtained at very high altitudes provided the relight is accomplished before the compressor rpm has decreased appreciably. In the event of a flame-out at airspeeds and altitudes above the "Probable Start Region" on the chart, the following procedure should be tried immediately a flame-out at high altitude occurs:

(a)   Close the appropriate throttle to the idle position.

(b)   Press the relight button for 20 seconds and watch for an increase in turbine outlet temperature which indicates a relight.

5.   If the above procedure is unsuccessful proceed as follows:

(a)   Throttle lever to cut-off.

(b)   Windmill the engine for 20-30 seconds to dry out surplus fuel.

(c)   Fuel Control Selector - NORM (EMERG if a primary fuel system failure is suspected).

(d)   Adjust the IAS and altitude to within the "Normal Windmilling Start Range" (Fig. 3-1).

(e)   Advance throttle lever to idle and at the same time press and hold the relight button for 20 seconds.

(f)   Watch for an increase in turbine outlet temperature which indicates a relight.

(g)   When turbine outlet temperature has settled down, open the throttle lever to the desired position and resume normal flight.

FLYING CONTROLS - EMERGENCY PROCEDURES

PILOT INDICATION	PROBABLE CAUSE	IMMEDIATE ACTION	FURTHER ACTION	REMARKS
Master amber plus Left Hand LFY CONT HYD warning light. Plus EMERG DAMP and R/P AXIS OUT	Loss of hydraulic pressure in 'B' system	Reduce speed	Land as soon as possible	
Master amber Right Hand FLY CONT HYD warning light.	Loss of hydraulic press in 'A' system	Ensure mode of flying control remains in NORMAL. Land as soon as possible.		
TWO ENGINE FAIL (at least one engine windmilling). Master RED and AMBER plus LH and RH FLY CONT HYD. (Provided airspeed is less than Mach .4 @ S/L or .85 @ 55,000'). EMERG DAMP, R/P AXIS OUT		(1) Maintain airspeed above 250 knots EAS. OR Select RAM AIR TURBINE switch ON (Speed below 350 knots) if fitted. (2) Check that the emergency alternator is operating (i.e. emerg damp system, J4 Comp., artificial horizon, IFF).	Proceed to relight one engine.	

FLYING CONTROLS - EMERGENCY PROCEDURES (Cont'd)

PILOT INDICATION	PROBABLE CAUSE	IMMEDIATE ACTION	FURTHER ACTION	REMARKS
Master amber plus EMERG DAMP plus R/P AXIS OUT	Flight Limits Exceeded (a) Sideslip in excess of 10° and/or (b) Excessive transverse acceleration	Reduce manoeuvre	Re-engage normal mode when manoeuvre completed	
Master amber plus R/P AXIS OUT.	Flight Limits Exceeded (a) Roll rate in excess of 159°/sec. OR (b) Pitch 'g' in excess of 4-1/2 g to 5 g. OR Both (a) and (b) combined	Reduce manoeuvre	Re-engage normal mode when manoeuvre completed. Check "R/P AXIS OUT" light goes out.	
Master amber plus DAMP OUT plus EMERG DAMP and R/P AXIS OUT	(a) Change over was made to EMERGENCY mode, but the 'A' hydraulic system was unserviceable. OR (b) Damper power switch is OFF (c) Damping not engaged.	(a) Re-engage normal mode if possible. (b) Select damper power ON. (c) Engage normal damping.	(a) Land as soon as possible. (b) and (c) NIL.	Loss of stability in yaw at high speeds. Controllable at low speeds with no damping.

FLYING CONTROLS - EMERGENCY PROCEDURES (Cont'd)

PILOT INDICATION	PROBABLE CAUSE	IMMEDIATE ACTION	FURTHER ACTION	REMARKS
Considerable force required to move control column	Seized elevator trim unit or seized parallel servo	Overcome fault by force on stick. Select Disengage on stick button, if not effective, select ELEV TRIM DISENGAGE	Reduce speed. If selecting ELEV TRIM DISENGAGE cured the condition, pilot may reengage into normal mode. Land as soon as possible.	
Any unusual elevator movement not commanded by pilot in NORM or EMERG mode	Runaway elevator trim motor or runaway parallel servo	Overcome fault by force on stick. Select Disengage on stick button. If not effective, select ELEV TRIM DISENGAGE	Reduce speed. If selecting ELEV TRIM DISENGAGE cured the condition, pilot may reengage into normal mode.	

ELECTRICAL SYSTEM EMERGENCY PROCEDURES

PILOT INDICATION	PROBABLE CAUSE	IMMEDIATE ACTION	FURTHER ACTION	REMARKS
Master amber plus LH or RH ALTERNATOR FAIL warning light (DC FAIL warning light will always illuminate with the above)	(1) Failure of the electrical generating system	(1) Move appropriate ALTERNATOR switch to RESET and back to ON.	(1) If ALTERNATOR FAIL and DC FAIL lights go out, so will the master amber light go out. - No further action required. If ALTERNATOR FAIL light goes out and DC FAIL remains on (with master amber remaining on) press DC RESET button. If reset is accomplished, both lights will go out. If ALTERNATOR FAIL light does not go out - move appropriate ALTERNATOR switch OFF. PRESS TO RESET master amber.	
	(2) One-engine flame-out	(2) Carry out engine relight procedure	(2) No further action. When engine starts, the warning lights should go out.	

ELECTRICAL SYSTEM EMERGENCY PROCEDURES (Cont'd)

PILOT INDICATION	PROBABLE CAUSE	IMMEDIATE ACTION	FURTHER ACTION	REMARKS
Master amber plus LH and RH ALTERNATOR FAIL lights. (Will be accompanied by the DC FAIL light and BATT USE light.	(1) Flame-out of both engines (2) Failure of both electrical-generating systems	(1) Refer to two-engine flame-out procedure, para 3-2. (2) Move both ALTERNATOR switches to RESET and back to ON.	(2) Refer to one alternator failure above. BATT USE light will go out when DC is reset.	Emergency AC power will automatically be supplied by the emergency alternator. The battery will supply emergency DC power.
Master amber plus DC FAIL	Failure of one TRU	Press DC RESET button.	If DC FAIL light goes out (master amber will also go out). - No further action required. If DC FAIL light does not go out PRESS TO RESET master amber. The other TRU will maintain the DC services less the landing and taxi lights	

ELECTRICAL SYSTEM EMERGENCY PROCEDURES (Cont'd)

PILOT INDICATION	PROBABLE CAUSE	IMMEDIATE ACTION	FURTHER ACTION	REMARKS
Master amber plus DC FAIL and BATT USE	Failure of both TRUs	Press DC RESET button	If one TRU resets, the BATT USE light will go out - PRESS TO RESET master amber. If both TRUs reset, the DC FAIL, BATT USE and master amber light will go out. If all lights remain on - PRESS TO RESET master amber. Land as soon as possible.	<u>CAUTION</u> (Limited DC loads are now taken from the aircraft battery.

FUEL SYSTEM EMERGENCY PROCEDURES

PILOT INDICATION	PROBABLE CAUSE	IMMEDIATE ACTION	FURTHER ACTION	REMARKS
Master amber, plus LH or RH ENG FUEL PRESS warning light	Relevant booster pump inoperative (Pressure has dropped below 18 psi)	NONE. Tank pressurization will maintain sufficient fuel delivery to the engine pumps to maintain military rating.	Throttle back affected engine until light goes out. PRESS-TO-RESET master amber.	Excessive engine operation in this condition is detrimental to engine pumps, particularly after high speed operations, due to temperature effects. Crossfeed from the side with most fuel, when one sub-system is empty.
Master amber plus FUEL PROP warning light. In flight). (FUEL LOW light NOT on).	Inoperative fuselage transfer pump OR A transfer pump has lost its prime	Climb the aircraft above 10° nose-up for 15 seconds. If it occurs on a descent, open up the engines momentarily to military rating.	If the light goes out, no further action. If light remains on, avoid sustained operation at high altitudes. Fuselage tank fuel may not be used in proportion to other tanks, particularly at high altitudes. PRESS-TO-RESET master amber.	Fuel quantity should be closely monitored. When fuel quantity on one side reaches approximately 2300 lb., the remaining fuselage tank contents may not be usable at the altitude of operation. However, it will be usable at sea level.

FUEL SYSTEM EMERGENCY PROCEDURES (Cont'd)

PILOT INDICATION	PROBABLE CAUSE	IMMEDIATE ACTION	FURTHER ACTION	REMARKS
Master amber plus FUEL PROP warning light. (LH or RH FUEL LOW warning light on temporarily.	Relevant fuel flow proportioner seized.	NONE Automatic control of the fuel C of G has ceased.	Avoid violent manoeuvres. PRESS-TO-RESET master amber.	
Master amber plus LH or RH FUEL LOW warning light plus FUEL PROP warning light.	Aircraft fuel supply low on that side. (Light illuminates when fuel is down to 740 lb on that side). OR Stalled flow proportioner.	Prepare to land at nearest airfield. Throttle back affected engine until light goes out.	(1) Cross check fuel supply with content gauges. (2) Crossfeed when one sub-system is empty. PRESS-TO-RESET master amber.	
One engine failure (Engine will not relight).		Carry out engine fail procedure (See para 3-1). Throttle lever of failed engine to cut-off.	Maintain fuel weight on each side approximately equal by alternating the fuel CROSSFEED between NORMAL and the failed engine side during the flight.	Adequate aileron control is available to maintain flying control with an unbalanced fuel condition. It is preferable however, to maintain the fuel quantity in each side approximately equal, due to shift in C of G which may occur.

FUEL SYSTEM EMERGENCY PROCEDURES (Cont'd)

PILOT INDICATION	PROBABLE CAUSE	IMMEDIATE ACTION	FURTHER ACTION	REMARKS
ON GROUND Master amber plus FUEL PROP warning light.	(1) Refuelling access doors not properly closed or defective access door micro-switch. (2) Master refuelling switch inadvertently left on. (3) A seized fuel flow proportioner (If engines are running).	Inform ground crew.		

AIR CONDITIONING AND PRESSURIZATION EMERGENCY PROCEDURES

PILOT INDICATION	PROBABLE CAUSE	IMMEDIATE ACTION	FURTHER ACTION	REMARKS
Master Amber plus AIR COND FAIL warning light	On Ground (1) Low engine rpm on hot day taxi. In Air (2) Cooling turbine outlet air exceeds 80"F. (3) Lack of water in air-to-water heat exchanger. (4) Seized Turbine.	On Ground (1) Increase engine rpm In Air Reduce power - if light does not go out then:- Speed below Mach 1.2 Select AIR SUPPLY switch - EMERG	In Air Reduce altitude. Land as soon as possible. PRESS TO RESET master amber	
Master amber plus CABIN PRESSURE warning light. (Check with cabin pressure gauge).	Cabin pressure has reached the equivalent of 31,000 feet, +1800 feet or higher. (1) Failure of the canopy seal. (2) Cabin pressure switch on DUMP. (3) Air supply switch on EMERG or OFF. (4) Sticking open of cabin pressure safety valve or controller failed. (5) See below.	(a) Throttle back engines (b) Open speed brakes (c) Descend to 35,000 feet or below	PRESS TO RESET master caution	

AIR CONDITIONING AND PRESSURIZATION EMERGENCY PROCEDURES (Cont'd)

PILOT INDICATION	PROBABLE CAUSE	IMMEDIATE ACTION	FURTHER ACTION	REMARKS
Master amber plus CABIN PRESSURE Warning light. (Check with cabin pressure gauge).	(5) Sticking open of outflow valve or controller.			
LH or RH ENG BLEED warning light (RED) (No master warning light indication).	(1) Leaking of hot engine bleed air occurring OR (2) Failure of pressure reducing valve.	Select LH OFF or RH OFF, depending on which light illuminates) on the ENG BLEED AIR toggle switch.	Warning light will go out when condition is relieved. Switch must be maintained in the LH OFF or RH OFF position while airborne.	
Master amber plus EQUIP O'HEAT warning light.	Equipment area temperature has exceeded 100°F.	If light on for short period - NONE. If light remains on select TEMP CONTROL switch to EMERG OFF.	PRESS-TO-RESET master amber.	Light should go out, as the hot air is automatically shut off until the equipment area temperature has reduced to 60°F.
Cabin uncomfortably hot.	Cabin temperature control valve failed.	Select TEMP CONTROL switch to EMERG OFF.		

ENGINES - EMERGENCY PROCEDURES

PILOT INDICATION	PROBABLE CAUSE	IMMEDIATE ACTION	FURTHER ACTION	REMARKS
Master amber plus LH or RH ROTOR O'SPEED warning light on momentarily	Temporary over-speeding of a low pressure compressor.	NONE		Occurs when the afterburner is lit or shut down.
Master amber plus LH or RH ROTOR O'SPEED warning light on steadily.	Malfunction of a low pressure compressor overspeed limiter.	Reduce engine power until light goes out.	Maintain warning light out by reduced power and speed.	
Master amber plus LH or RH FUEL PRESS warning light.	See FUEL SYSTEM EMERGENCIES			
Low turbine discharge temperature.	Afterburner nozzle remaining open after closing down afterburner.	Retard throttle lever out of afterburner range on quadrant.		
Low turbine discharge temperature	Afterburner fails to light up, but nozzle opens.	Retard throttle lever out of afterburner range on quadrant.		
Master amber plus ICE warning light.	Ice detectors icing and de-icing.	If engines are operating at relatively high thrust - no further action. If descending or engines are operating at relatively low (See below)	Further action depends upon icing conditions.	(The interval between the lights going on and off will denote the severity of the icing conditions. Short interval will denote severe icing.)

ENGINES - EMERGENCY PROCEDURES (Cont'd)

PILOT INDICATION	PROBABLE CAUSE	IMMEDIATE ACTION	FURTHER ACTION	REMARKS
		Thrust, open up engines occasionally to provide additional heat	See EO 05-1-1 Pilot's Operating Instructions - General	
One engine flame-out occurring for no apparent cause.	Malfunction of hydro-mechanical fuel flow control unit.	Select ENG FUEL switch to EMERG.	Carry out engine re-light procedure.	Complete the flight in EMERG fuel. Ensure turbine discharge temperature does not exceed limits.
Rapid rise in turbine discharge temperature for no apparent cause.	Malfunction of hydro-mechanical fuel flow control unit.	Select ENG FUEL switch to EMERG.	Check that the EMERG selection corrects the condition.	Check that the EMERG selection corrects the condition.
Rough engine operation	Malfunction of hydro-mechanical fuel flow control unit.	Select ENG FUEL switch to EMERG.	Check that the EMERG selection corrects the condition.	Complete the flight in EMERG fuel. Ensure turbine discharge temp. does not exceed limits.
One engine or two engine flame out. (Possibly through excessive manoeuvring causing interrupted air flow to engine inlet).	Compressor stall.	Throttle to idle and attempt an immediate relight of one engine.		(See Part 3, para 2.)
Master amber plus LH or RH OIL PRESS warning light.	Engine oil pressure has reduced to 25 psi or below.	Shut down affected engine.	Reduce speed in order to lower windmilling rpm of affected engine. PRESS TO RESET Master amber.	

EMERGENCY LANDINGS

6.   All emergency landings, either on prepared or unprepared surfaces, should be made with the landing gear down. The extended gear, even on reasonably rough terrain, helps to absorb the initial shock. The inherent nose high landing attitude will result in a severe "slap" into the ground if the tail section is permitted to take the initial shock of a wheels up landing.

LANDING GEAR EMERGENCY PROCEDURES

General

7.   The procedure to be adopted is dependent upon the indications given by the UTIL HYD warning light and the landing gear position indicator. It should be noted that once the emergency nitrogen system has been used, the landing gear cannot be reselected up, therefore the following procedure should be carried out in the sequence given.

Hydraulic Pressure Normal

8.   If the UTIL HYD warning light is not illuminated, there should be sufficient hydraulic pressure to open the doors and unlock the landing gear.

9.   If, after a normal down selection the indicators show that the gear is still locked up, a fault in the selection circuit is indicated. In this case, proceed as follows:

(a) Re-select UP and DOWN a number of times.

NOTE

If the BATT USE light is illuminated, the landing gear selector valve is inoperative. (See Part 1, para 44 NOTE.) In this case the action in sub-para (a)above will have no effect and is unnecessary.

(b) If this fails, push the thumb latch button and move the landing gear handle fully down to the EMERGENCY EXTENSION position.

10.   If, after a normal down selection, the indicators show a between-locks indication for one or more of the legs, an indicator fault or a mechanical fault is indicated. In this case, proceed as follows:

(a) Attempt to lock the gear down by yawing to the left and right to open the doors and shake the legs down by applying positive 'g' in the pitching plane. Waggling the wings and accelerating the aircraft to 250 knots EAS may also help to lock the gear down.

(b) If this does not obtain a locked down indication, check with the control tower to see if the gear appears to be locked down.

(c) If the gear is not locked down, re-select UP and make a wheels-up landing.

Insufficient Hydraulic Pressure

11.   If the UTIL HYD warning light is illuminated there will probably be insufficient hydraulic pressure to unlock the doors and landing gear locks. (See para 12.) In this case use the EMERGENCY EXTENSION selection.

BRAKE EMERGENCY PROCEDURES

Emergency Operation of the Brakes

12.   Two accumulators in the utility hydraulic system supply emergency brake pressure automatically upon failure of the normal supply. Indication that the normal supply has failed (pressure reduced to 1000 psi or less) is given by the illumination of the UTIL HYD warning light. (See para 11.)

13.   When a landing after a utility system failure the brakes should be applied sparingly, pumping should be avoided, and every effort should be made to complete the landing run with as few applications of the brakes as is possible.

CAUTION

After completion of the landing run do not taxi the aircraft, even though brake pressure may still be available. Shut down the engines.

14.   Should the pressure in the accumulators fall below 1600 psi, the light on the warning panel marked EMERG BRAKE HYD will illuminate. This light warns the pilot that the aircraft brakes will be ineffective upon landing.

Engine Thrust at Idle RPM

15.   Engine thrust at idle rpm is comparatively high. In a case of brake failure, the engines should be stopped as soon as possible.

AIRFRAME AND ENGINE ICING

General

16.   The anti-icing and de-icing systems are entirely automatic. No manual controls are provided. If the automatic functions fail during icing conditions the aircraft should be operated as laid down in Pilot's Operating Instructions General EO 05-1-1.

Engine Anti-Icing

17.   Only intermittent use of high rpm during descent under severe icing conditions is necessary. At the relatively high thrust setting used during climb or cruise, the hot air to the compressor inlet section of the engine is adequate to prevent ice formation.

ACTION IN THE EVENT OF FIRE

18.   Should the master RED warning light on the instrument panel illuminate, carry out the following procedure:

(a)   Check the location of the fire on the FIRE panel by means of the illuminated bulb.

(b)   If an engine fire is indicated - retard the throttle lever of the appropriate engine to the cut-off position.

(c)   Switch off the appropriate LP cock.

(d)   Press the illuminated bulb on the FIRE panel.

(e)   If the fire is extinguished, the light on the warning panel will go out.

(f)   If the warning panel light does not go out, lift the guard and select the SECOND SHOT switch on.

NOTE

The toggle switch is used only to give a second shot to the same compartment. If two separate fires occur, pressing the appropriate two warning lights will provide one shot to each compartment.

ABANDONING THE AIRCRAFT

General

19.   The aircraft may be abandoned by means of the ejection seats at a minimum airspeed of 80 knots IAS at ground level.

Pilot Preliminaries

20.   If it becomes necessary to abandon the aircraft, the following procedure should be adopted:

(a)   Reduce the aircraft speed, if possible.

(b)   Order the navigator to eject or, if intercommunication has failed, operate the NAV BAIL OUT signal switch. Check that the green NAV BAIL OUT light illuminates.

Navigator

21.   After receiving the verbal order to eject, or if the BAIL OUT warning light illuminates and the signal horn sounds during inter-communication failure, proceed as follows:

(a)   Acknowledge a verbal order.

(b)   Ensure that the head is correctly located on the headrest, and lean fully back.

(c)   Grasp the overhead hiring handle in both hands, ensuring that the palms of the hands face to the rear.

(d)   Maintain the head hard back against the headrest and the arms and hands close to the chest, then pull the firing handle and face screen firmly down over the face. The canopy will open immediately. Seat ejection will take place as soon as the canopy is fully open.

CAUTION

The overhead firing handle must be pulled straight down over the face
and not outwards away from the face.

(e)   Should the canopy fail to open, pull the EMERGENCY CANOPY OPEN lever fully to the rear. Replace the hand in its previous position with relation to the face blind as rapidly as possible. Ejection will occur immediately the canopy is in the emergency-open position, which provides very little time to return the hand to the face blind.

NOTE

If, for any reason, the overhead firing handle cannot be operated, pull the
alternate firing handle (located between the knees) fully upwards by
grasping it with both hands, one hand over the other.

Pilot

22.   After the navigator has left the aircraft (indicated by the green NAV BAIL OUT light being extinguished) proceed as follows:

(a)   Ensure that the head is correctly located on the headrest, and lean fully back.

(b)   Grasp the overhead firing handle with both hands ensuring that the palms of the hands face to the rear.

(c)   Maintain the head hard back against the headrest and the arms and hands close to the chest, then pull the firing handle and face screen firmly down over the face. The canopy will open immediately. Seat ejection will take place as soon as the canopy is fully open.

CAUTION

The overhead firing handle must be pulled down straight over the face
and not outwards away from the face.

(e)   Should the canopy fail to open, pull the EMERGENCY CANOPY OPEN lever fully to the rear. Replace the hand in its previous position with relation to the face blind as rapidly as possible. Ejection will occur immediately the canopy is in the emergency-open position, which provides very little time to return the hand to the face blind.

NOTE

If, for any reason, the overhead firing handle cannot be operated, pull the alternative firing handle (located between the knees) fully upwards by grasping it with both hands, one hand over the other.

Manual Release

23.   If, for any reason, the seat does not eject or, when ejected, the automatic parachute opening gear does not function, provision is made to disconnect the parachute and parachute harness from the seat and enable the occupant to operate the parachute manually as follows:

(a)   Pull on the outer 'D' ring.

(b)   Release the spring catch on the manual override lever on the RH side of the seat pan and move the lever fully to the rear.

(c)   Leave the aircraft or seat.

(d)   Pull the ripcord 'D' ring.

EMERGENCY CANOPY OPENING ON THE GROUND

From Inside the Cockpit

24.   In the event that either canopy cannot be opened by the normal method and an emergency exists, the lever marked EMERGENCY CANOPY OPEN, located on the RH side of each cockpit, should be pulled fully back.

From Outside the Cockpit

25.   In an emergency, should either crew member be unable to operate his emergency canopy opening handle, provision is made for these handles to be operated from outside the aircraft. A door, located on the RH side of the aircraft below the pilot's cockpit, is marked in red letters EMERGENCY CANOPY OPENING -PUSH TO OPEN - STAND BACK - PULL HANDLE. When the toggle handle attached to the lanyard is pulled, both canopies will be opened by cartridge firing.

WARNING

The canopies will be forced open very rapidly. Therefore all personnel should stand clear of the canopies when the lanyard is pulled.

Operating Data

ENGINE LIMITATIONS

PRINCIPAL LIMITATIONS

1.   The principal limitations of the Pratt and Whitney J-75 P3 engines are:

Condition	Maximum Observed Turbine Discharge Temp °C	Time Limit (Minutes)
MAXIMUM (With A/B)	610	Fifteen
MILITARY	610	Thirty
NORMAL RATED	540	UNRESTRICTED
CRUISE		
90% NORMAL RATED	540(max) 500(normal)	UNRESTRICTED
80% NORMAL RATED	540(max) 460(normal)	UNRESTRICTED
70% NORMAL RATED	540(max) 410(normal)	UNRESTRICTED
IDLE	340	UNRESTRICTED
STARTING	600	MOMENTARY
TRANSIENT	625	One

FLYING LIMITATIONS

2.   The following speeds and limitations apply to the ARROW 1 aircraft when fully cleared to its design specification. Until such clearance is obtained, the applicable aircraft design certificate must be studied prior to flight to obtain the overriding limitations to those given below:

(a)   Maximum Permissible Speeds

Maximum Design Speed	-	700 Knots EAS or Mach 2.0 (Lowest limit to apply)
Extending or Retracting Landing Gear	-	250 Knots EAS
Extending Speed Brakes	-	No Limit
Parabrake Selection in ground contact)	-	185 Knots EAS (All wheels
Cross-wind component	-	30 Knots

(b)   Crew Ejection

Maximum Speed	-	No structural limit
Minimum Speed	-	80 Knots at ground level

(c)   Angle of Attack

Maximum Indicated Angle	-	15° (in level flight) 1/2° less for each incremental 'g' imposed

(d)   Weights

Maximum Take-off	-	69,000 lb. (approx)
Maximum Landing	-	65,000 lb. (approx)

(e)   'G' Limits
'G' Limits are shown on Figs 4-1, 4-2 and 4-3
The maximum load factor in a rolling pull-out is two-thirds of the maximum
   allowable 'g' at that time.

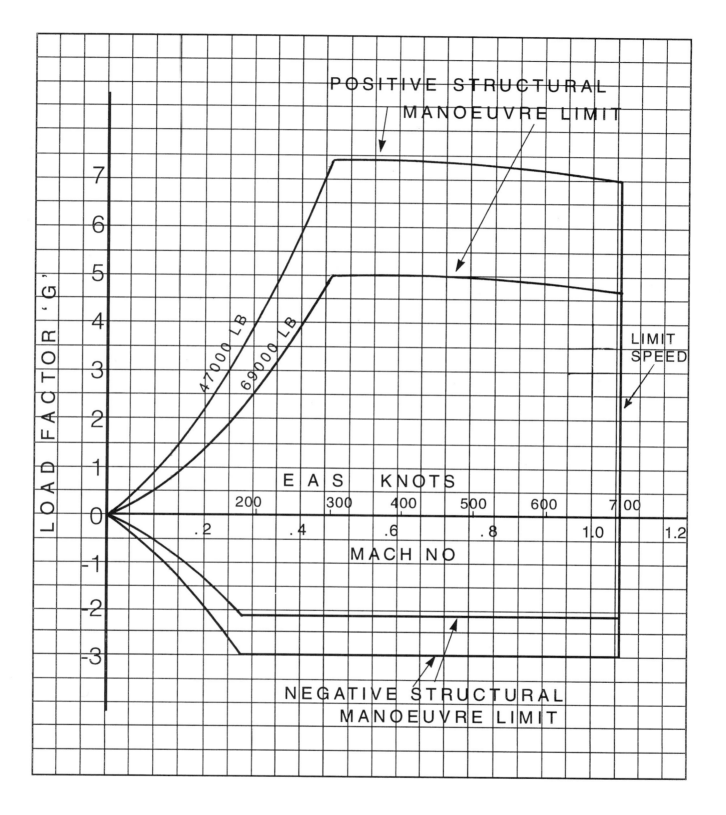

FIG 4-1 FLIGHT ENVELOPE - SEA LEVEL

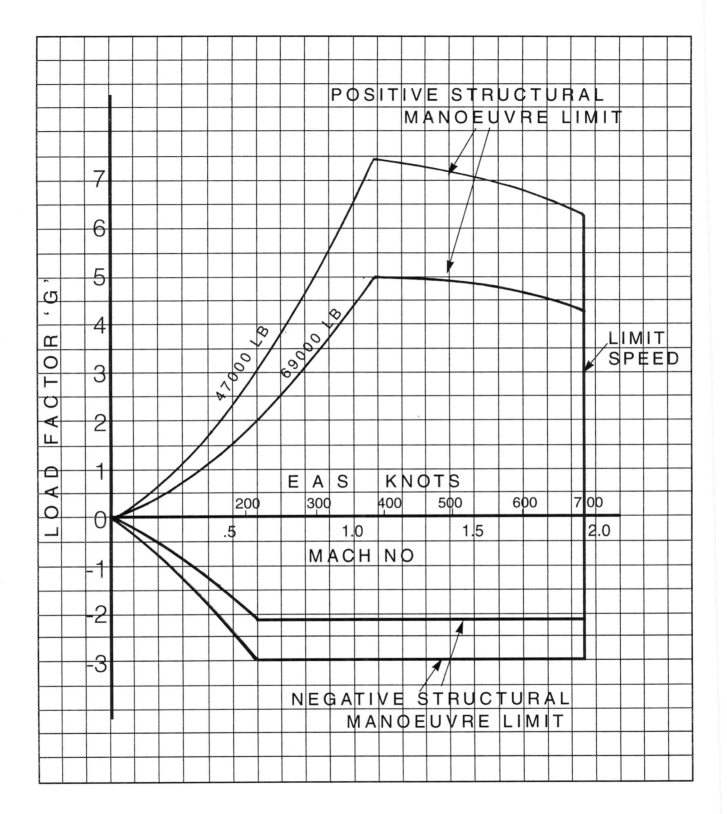

FIG 4-2 FLIGHT ENVELOPE - 30,000 FT

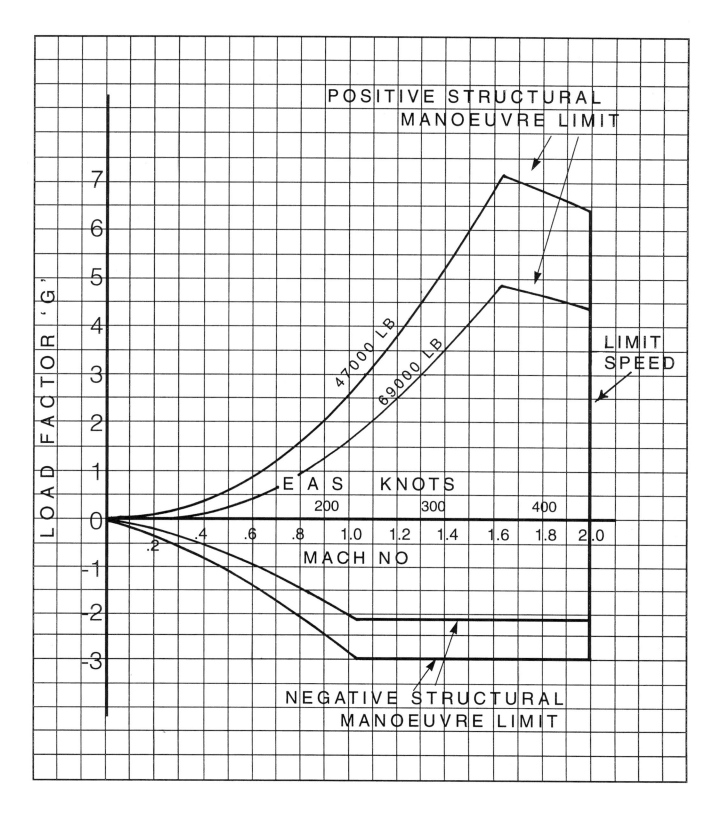

FIG 4-3 FLIGHT ENVELOPE - 50,000 FT

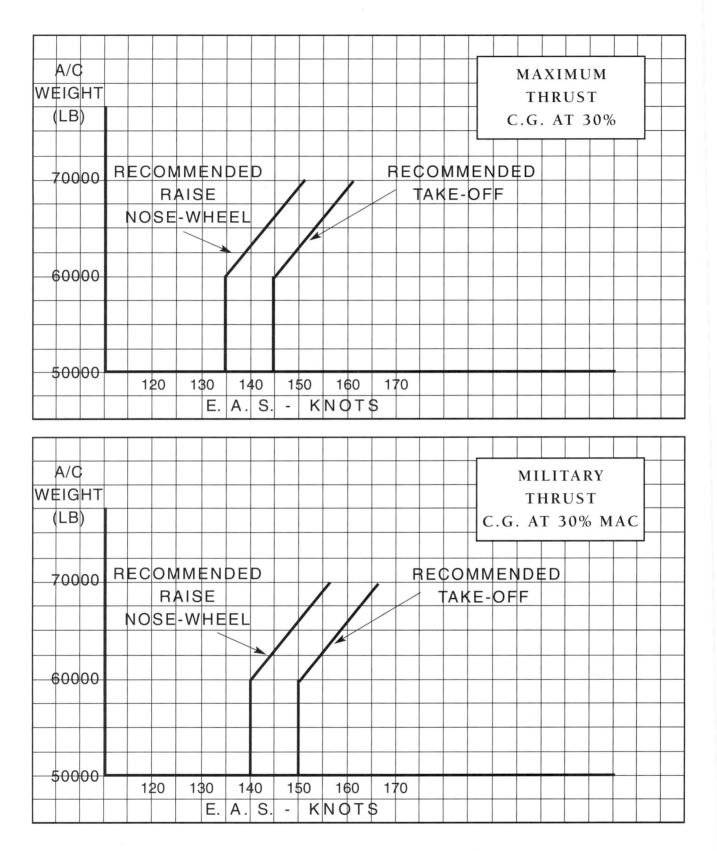

FIG 4-4 RECOMMENDED TAKE-OFF SPEEDS

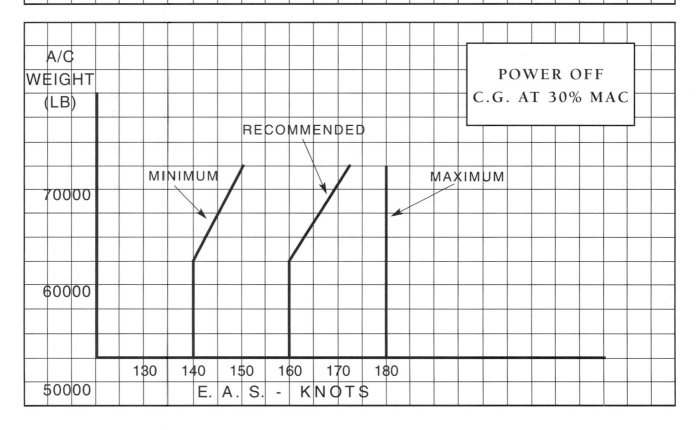

FIG 4-6 RECOMMENDED TOUCH-DOWN SPEEDS

AIRCRAFT ARROW 1	TAKE-OFF DISTANCES FEET (AT SEA LEVEL)				ENGINES J 75 - P 3	
A/C WEIGHT AT START OF T.O. (LB)	STANDARD DAY 15°C A/B ON		HOT DAY 38°C A/B ON		STANDARD DAY 15°C NO A/B	
	GROUND RUN	CLEAR 50'	GROUND RUN	CLEAR 50'	GROUND RUN	CLEAR 50'
50,000	1450	2585	1750	3540	2450	5250
55,000	1600	2900	2050	4180	2720	6210
60,000	1780	3260	2250	4775	3100	7480
65,000	2120	3990	2950	6230	3800	9950
(70,000)	2630	4965	3530	7800	4450	13210

DATA AS OF: March 1958 (71/PERF/3)

BASED ON: Estimated Data

BASED ON: J P 4 FUEL

FIGURES HAVE NOT BEEN FLIGHT CHECKED.
INITIAL FLIGHT TESTS INDICATE THAT THE
DISTANCES MAY BE PESSIMISTIC.

FIG 4-7 TAKE-OFF DISTANCE CHART

AIRCRAFT ARROW	CLIMB CHART (At 527 KTS. T.A.S.) NO AFTERBURNER				ENGINES J75 - P 3
MILITARY THRUST - ENGINE START GROSS WT. - 60,000 LB.					
PRESSURE ALT.	TRUE A/S (KNOTS)	APPROPRIATE VALUES			RATE OF CLIMB
		FROM SEA LEVEL			
		FUEL (LB)	TIME (MIN)	DIST. (N.M.)	
Sea Level	527	0	0	0	10,500
5,000	527	236	0.48	4.3	10,500
10,000	527	471	1.02	8.8	8,850
15,000	527	706	1.63	14.2	7,550
20,000	527	940	2.32	20.4	6,200
25,000	527	1192	3.22	28.0	4.750
30,000	527	1480	4.43	38.7	3,200
35,000	527	1917	6.58	58.0	1,400
Start, Take-off and Accelerate to Climb Allowance		817	2.1	7.9	

DATA AS OF: Oct. 1957 (71/PERF/3)

BASED ON: Estimated Data

BASED ON: J P 4 Fuel

FIGURES HAVE NOT BEEN FLIGHT CHECKED

FIG 4-8 CLIMB CHART (NO A/B) - 60,000 LB

AIRCRAFT ARROW	CLIMB CHART (At 527 KTS. T.A.S.) NO AFTERBURNER			ENGINES J75 - P 3
MILITARY THRUST - ENGINE START GROSS WT. - 68,765 LB.				
PRESSURE ALT.	TRUE A/S (KNOTS)	APPROPRIATE VALUES FROM SEA LEVEL		RATE OF CLIMB
		FUEL (LB)	TIME (MIN)	DIST. (N.M.)	

PRESSURE ALT.	TRUE A/S (KNOTS)	FUEL (LB)	TIME (MIN)	DIST. (N.M.)	RATE OF CLIMB
Sea Level	527	0	0	0	9,100
5,000	527	273	0.57	5.0	8,600
10,000	527	546	1.18	10.2	7,450
15,000	527	827	1.88	16.5	6,300
20,000	527	1108	2.74	24.0	5,100
25,000	527	1403	3.81	33.4	3,850
30,000	527	1752	5.29	46.5	2,400
35,000	527	2360	8.29	73.4	500
Start, Take-off and Accelerate to Climb Allowance		946	2.5	9.9	

DATA AS OF: Oct. 1957 (71/PERF/3)

BASED ON: Estimated Data

BASED ON: J P 4 Fuel

FIGURES HAVE NOT BEEN FLIGHT CHECKED

FIG 4-9 CLIMB CHART (NO A/B) - 68,765 LB

AIRCRAFT ARROW 1		CLIMB CHART WITH AFTERBURNERS				ENGINES J 75 - P 3	
		MAXIMUM THRUST - ENGINE START GROSS WT. - 60,000 LB.					
PRESSURE ALT.	MACH NO.		APPROXIMATE VALUES FROM SEA LEVEL			RATE OF CLIMB	
	HIGH SPEED CLIMB	COMBAT CLIMB	FUEL	TIME (MIN)	DISTANCE (N.M.)		
Sea Level	.92	.92	0	0	0	37,000	
5,000	.92	.92	280	.16	1.0	35,000	
10,000	.92	.92	500	.30	2.5	32,000	
15,000	.92	.92	750	.45	4.0	28,000	
20,000	.92	.92	1000	.64	5.5	24,000	
25,000	.92	.92	1200	.86	7.0	20,000	
30,000	.92	.92	1450	1.10	9.5	16,000	
30,000	-	1.5 (accel)	-	-	-	-	nil
35,000	.92	1.5	1700	1.5	12.5	11,000	14,500
40,000	.92	1.5	2000	2.0	17.0	7,000	11,500
45,000	.92	1.5	2500	3.0	26.0	3,000	6,000
47,000	-	1.5	-	4.2	51.0	-	4,000
50,000	-	1.5	-	5.2	66.0	-	1,500
51,000	-	1.5	-	5.9	76.0	-	500
30,000				2.7	30.0		
35,000				3.0	33.5		
40,000				3.2	38.0		
45,000				3.8	46.0		
Start. Take-off and Accelerate to Climb Allowance			1643	1.39	4.47		

DATE AS OF: Oct. 1957 (71/PERF/3) Notes:
BASED ON: Estimated Data
BASED ON: J P 4 Fuel
FIGURES HAVE NOT BEEN FLIGHT CHECKED

FIG 4-10 CLIMB CHART (WITH A/B) - 60,000 LB

AIRCRAFT ARROW 1 **GROSS WT. 68,765 LB.** **CLIMB CHART — WITH AFTERBURNERS** **ENGINES MAX THRUST J 75 - P 3g119**

APPROXIMATE VALUES

PRESSURE ALT.	MACH NO. HIGH SPEED CLIMB	MACH NO. COMBAT CLIMB	FUEL (LB)	FROM SEA LEVEL TIME (MIN)	FROM SEA LEVEL DISTANCE (N.M.)	RATE OF CLIMB
Sea Level	.92	.92	0	0	0	32,000
5,000	.92	.92	300	.15	1.5	30,500
10,000	.92	.92	600	.35	2.5	28,000
15,000	.92	.92	860	.50	4.5	24,800
20,000	.92	.92	1100	.75	6.5	21,000
25,000	.92	.92	1400	1.0	8.5	17,400
30,000	.92	.92	1700	1.3	11.0	13,600

PRESSURE ALT.	HIGH SPEED CLIMB (Mach)	COMBAT CLIMB (Mach)	FUEL (LB) High Speed	FUEL (LB) Combat	TIME (MIN) High Speed	TIME (MIN) Combat	DISTANCE (N.M.) High Speed	DISTANCE (N.M.) Combat	RATE OF CLIMB High Speed	RATE OF CLIMB Combat
30,000	-	1.5 (accel)	-	3500	-	3.0	-	31.5	-	nil
35,000	.92	1.5	2000	3900	1.75	3.3	15.0	36.0	10,000	-
40,000	.92	1.5	2300	4250	2.4	3.7	21.0	40.5	5,200	9,500
45,000	.92	1.5	3100	4800	4.0	4.4	35.0	50.0	1,000	4,500
47,000	-	1.5	-	5100	-	4.9	-	58.0	-	2,700
49,000	-	1.5	-	5750	-	5.9	-	72.0	-	900

Start, Take-off and Accelerate to Climb Allowance	FUEL 1879	TIME 1,529	DISTANCE 5,303

DATE AS OF: Oct. 1957 (71/PERF/3)
BASED ON: Estimated Data
BASED ON: J P 4 Fuel

FIG 4-11 CLIMB CHART (WITH A/B) - 68,765 LB

AIRCRAFT ARROW 1	FUEL FLOW AT MACH 0.92 AND MACH 1.5 IN LB/MIN/ENGINE								ENGINES J 75 - P 3	
ALTITUDE FT.	AIRCRAFT WEIGHT LB.										
	45,000		50,000		55,000		60,000		65,000	
	Mach .92	Mach 1.5	Mach .92	Mach 1.5	Mach .92	Mach 1.5	Mach .92	Mach 1.5	Mach .92	Mach 1.5
25,000	69.2	-	72.3	-	75.5	-	79.1	-	83.3	-
30,000	62.6	-	65.9	-	70.8	-	76.9	-	82.3	-
35,000	58.0	465.0	63.1	470.0	70.0	472.0	78.6	472.0	87.9	476.0
40,000	58.0	382.0	64.5	384.0	73.9	386.4	-	386.4	-	387.8
45,000	57.7	303.5	69.2	305.5	-	307.5	-	310.5	-	316.0

DATE AS OF: Oct. 1957 (71/PERF/3)   Notes: (1) 45" Divergent ejector used.
BASED ON: Estimated Data
BASED ON: J P 4 Fuel   (2) Fuel flow is increased by 5%

FIGURES HAVE NOT BEEN FLIGHT CHECKED

FIG 4-12 FUEL FLOW CHART

AIRCRAFT ARROW 1	LANDING DISTANCE FEET (WITH PARABRAKE AND DIVEBRAKES)		ENGINES J 75 - P 3
GROSS WT. LB.	APPROACH E.A.S. KNOTS	HARD SURFACE RUNWAY - NO WIND - TEMP 15°C - ENGINES IDLE	
		AT SEA LEVEL	
		GROUND RUN	CLEAR 50'
50,000	180	4,850	7,500
55,000	180	5,100	7,680
60,000	180	5,500	8,040
65,000	187	6,100	8,680
70,000	194	6,780	9,420

DATA AS OF: March 1958 (71/PERF/3)

BASED ON: Estimated Data

BASED ON: J P 4 Fuel

Notes: (1) Parabrake and Brakes Effective at 90% of Touch-down Speed.

(2) Without Anti-Skid Units

FIGURES HAVE NOT BEEN FLIGHT CHECKED INITIAL FLIGHT TESTS INDICATE THAT THE DISTANCES MAY BE PESSIMISTIC.

FIG 4-13 LANDING DISTANCE CHART - WITH PARABRAKE

AIRCRAFT ARROW 1	LANDING DISTANCE FEET (WITH PARABRAKE AND DIVEBRAKES)		ENGINES J 75 - P 3	
GROSS WT. LB.	APPROACH E.A.S. KNOTS	BRAKING SPEED E.A.S. KNOTS	HARD SURFACE RUNWAY - NO WIND - TEMP 15°C - ENGINES IDLE	
			AT SEA LEVEL	
			GROUND RUN	CLEAR 50'
50,000	180	144	7,500	10,200
55,000	180	144	7,680	10,460
60,000	180	136	8,040	11,070
65,000	187	127	8,680	13,050
70,000	194	120	9,420	15,490

DATA AS OF: March 1958 (71/PERF/11)

BASED ON: Estimated Data

BASED ON: J P 4 Fuel

Notes: (1) Brakes Effective at 90% of Touch-down Speed except above 55,000 lb., where braking is shown above to avoid exceeding the Brake Energy Limitation.

(2) Without Anti-Skid Units

FIGURES HAVE NOT BEEN FLIGHT CHECKED INITIAL FLIGHT TESTS INDICATE THAT THE DISTANCES MAY BE PESSIMISTIC.

FIG 4-14 LANDING DISTANCE CHART - WITHOUT PARABRAKE

AVRO ARROW FLIGHT TEST SUMMARY

THE FLIGHT TEST PROGRAM

The actual flights conducted on the AVRO Arrow were restricted to the Mark I version. Four pilots were checked out on the aircraft and each would have studied the pilot's operating instructions you have just reviewed. However, only one observer, on one flight, flew in the backseat. The four pilots were Jan Zurakowski, Peter Cope, Spud Potocki and Flight Lieutenant Jack Woodman. The first three were AVRO company employees while Flt Lt Woodman was obviously a RCAF test pilot.

As can be seen in the next section, the flight test program was originally scheduled as an eight-phase program. The first series of tests were designed to evaluate the basic handling qualities of the aircraft, to evaluate the flight control system, to check instrumentation and telemetry, and to confirm the safety of flight under potentially adverse conditions. The initial series of flights involved pre-production testing and development employing the first five Mark I, aircraft which were equipped with the Pratt & Whitney J-75 engines. The 6th aircraft was to be the first Mark II version equipped with more powerful, Orenda-built, Iroquois engines.

Unfortunately, only a portion of the initial Phase I pre-production testing was completed. The first five aircraft flew a total of 64 flights for a total of 68 hours and 45 minutes flight time. Jan Zurakowski, the Chief Development Pilot for AVRO, had the honour of the inaugural flight on 25 March 1958. The initial flight was straightforward: Jan lifted off climbing to a maximum height of 10,000 feet at speeds up to 400 mph. After briefly flying over Malton at varying altitudes while checking the response of controls, engines and testing the undercarriage and air brakes, he returned for an uneventful landing. He "reported good flying qualities, no surprises, no trouble, and made the general comment, it handled very nicely." Less than a year later, on 07 Feb 59, both aircraft No 1 and 4 completed test flights. This ended up being the last day any Arrow aircraft left the ground.

The following is a summary of the initial tests and flights completed in this year-long period:

First engine runs	04 Dec 1957
First taxi trials	24 Dec 1957
First flight (a/c 25201)	25 Mar 1958
First flight (a/c 25202)	01 Aug 1958
First flight (a/c 25203)	22 Sep 1958
First flight (a/c 25204)	27 Oct 1958
First flight (a/c 25205)	11 Jan 1959
Final flight(s) (a/c 25201 & 25203)	19 Feb 1959

A summary of flights by aircraft tail number is as follows:

	No. of Flights	Flight Hours
25201	25	25 hr 40 min
25202	22	23 hr 40 min
25203	12	13 hr 30 min
25204	6	07 hr 0 min
25205	1	40 min
Total	66	70 hr 30 min *

*(7 hr 51 min at supersonic speed)

(A complete record of the individual flights by aircraft tail number can be found in Appendix 1)

Because of the maiden flight, Jan Zurakowski's name is indelibly attached to the Arrow. Although technically too old for "high performance" flying (the limit then was 40 years of age) Jan continued flying on the Arrow until he was 44.   Spud Potocki then took over most test flights and in fact had the most flight hours on the Arrow of any of the four test pilots. "The Arrow achieved supersonic speeds on its third flight and on its seventh flight reached MACH 1.5 at 50,000 feet. The highest speed recorded, MACH 1.97/1.98 was just short of the design max of MACH 2.0. About 95 per cent of the flight envelope was explored and handling was found to be generally satisfactory, although not flawless." "The aircraft flying characteristics were similar to that of other delta wing aircraft like the Javelin or Convair F-102, but the Arrow had a more positive response to control movement."

Jan Zurakowski had successfully completed Phase One of the test-flying program when Flt Lt Jack Woodman made his first familiarization and initial assessment flight. While Jan had stated the aircraft handled beautifully, Jack Woodman indicated that the Arrow at certain speeds and altitudes flew as well as any aircraft he had ever flown, but at other points control was very sensitive and difficult to fly. For instance, on his first flight he reported that at low and high indicated airspeeds, the aircraft behaved reasonably well, the controls were effective and responsive with the aircraft demonstrating positive stability. However, due to the sensitivity of the controls, the aircraft was difficult to fly accurately. At high MACH numbers, Woodman reported the transition from subsonic to supersonic speed was very smooth, with compressibility effects negligible and the sensitive control problem experienced at lower speeds and altitudes eliminated. "The aircraft, at supersonic speeds, was pleasant and easy to fly. During approach and landing, the handling characteristics were considered good; approach speed was 190 knots, touchdown was at 165 knots, drag chute was deployed at 155 knots, and the aircraft rolled the full length of the runway. Attitude during approach was approximately 10°, with good forward visibility."

On Jack Woodman's second flight, he "reported that the general handling characteristics of the Arrow MK I were much improved. . . .The yaw damper is now performing quite reliably, although turn co-ordination is questionable in some areas. The roll damper is not optimized as yet, and longitudinal control is sensitive at high IAS."

On his sixth and last flight, Woodman reported "longitudinal control to be positive with good response, and breakout force stick gradients to be very good. Lateral control was good, forces and gradients very good, and the erratic control in the rolling plane, encountered on the last flight, no longer there. Directionally, slip and skid was held to a minimum. At no time during the flight was there more than 1° of sideslip, and the problem of turn coordination appears to be eliminated at this point. Final approach to landing was at 175 knots and a 30 glideslope, attitude was approximately 12°, touchdown was at 160 knots, and the landing roll was estimate at 6000 to 6500 ft, with little or no braking." He further stated " that excellent progress was being made in the development of the Arrow."

Comments made by some of the other pilots who flew the Arrow include:

"The nosewheel can be lifted by very gentle movement of the stick at just over 120 knots."

"Unstick speed is about 170 knots with attitude of about 11°."

"Acceleration is rapid, with negligible correction required and no tendency to swing."

"Typical touchdown speed is a little over 165 knots."

"There is no indication of stalling at maximum angle of attack at 15°."

"Stability steadily improved with speed."

"Change of trim was negligible except in the transonic region, where small change of trim were required."

"In turns, stick force was moderate to light, but always positive, with no tendency to pitch up or lighten."

"In sideslip, the aircraft was a little touchy without the damper, but excellent with the damper engaged."

Two minor landing accidents marred the otherwise highly successful test flight program. The first involved aircraft 25201 flown by Jan Zurakowski. During the landing run, Jan realized that the aircraft was pulling to the left and he could not maintain direction. Suspecting that the braking parachute had not opened evenly, he jettisoned the chute but with no improvement. The aircraft exited the runway at a speed of approximately 30 mph and the undercarriage collapsed on contact with the soft ground.

"On investigation it was established that the left undercarriage leg had not completed the lowering cycle and during the landing run the wheels were at about a 45° angle to the direction of travel, producing a higher drag than the brakes on the right side could compensate for. With decrease of speed, rudder effectiveness decreased and the aircraft could not be prevented from changing direction."

"The second accident took place on aircraft No. 202, flown by Spud Potocki. During a landing roll all four wheels skidded and the tires burst. The pilot lost directional control and the aircraft ran off the runway, damaging the right undercarriage leg. The initial impression was that it was pilot error. The pilot was thought to have applied too much braking pressure and locked the wheels."

As it turned out, during this landing the aircraft experienced a small vibration on touch down which resulted in an inadvertent electrical signal to the stability augmentation system which in turn caused a full down deflection of the elevators. "The Arrow's elevators were large and when deflected fully down, acted as powerful flaps, increasing wing lift so much that only 20% of the aircraft weight was on the main wheels. The pilot was not aware of this and normal application of the brakes locked the wheels." Once the problem had been diagnosed, a solution was quickly engineered and the program resumed.

The test flights were all conducted from the AVRO facility in Malton, Ontario. The exception was one flight, which diverted to RCAF Station Trenton because of a problem on the runways in Malton. The aircraft overnighted in Trenton and was flown out the next day.

The weapon system intended for the AVRO Arrow was the ASTRA fire control system combined with Sparrow 2 radar guided missiles. The ASTRA 1 consisted of an integrated airborne system for electronic weapons, navigation and communication. It provided automatic flight control, airborne radar, telecommunications and navigation and special instrumentation and pilot displays and could operate in either fully automatic, semi-automatic or manual modes. The entire system was to be developed by R.C.A Victor, Honeywell Controls Ltd and Computing Devices of Canada Ltd. It was to have been extremely sophisticated but unfortunately it also turned out to be extremely expensive and difficult to develop. The ASTRA and Sparrow programs were eventually cancelled even in advance of the Arrow program itself.

None of the first five aircraft were equipped with an armament system. Instead each of these aircraft was equipped with a sophisticated data acquisition system. "The Arrow data acquisition and handling system was composed of an airborne multi-channel recorder (magnetic tape), phono panel, oscillograph, an airborne radio telemetry link, a mobile telemetry receiving station, and a mobile data reduction unit. The aircraft armament bay, which was a removable self-contained unit, was used to house all of the airborne instrumentation."

This instrumentation system proved to be a "constant source of trouble during the Arrow test program. "During the first series of flights, the system was plagued with a number problems that were probably due to the thousands of wires and connections running to the instrument pack…these problems were never really resolved, and many a flight was delayed because of this system."

On the day the Arrow program was cancelled, Arrow No. 6 (25206), the first of the Iroquois-equipped Mk IIs, was 98% complete and was an estimated two weeks away from its first flight. "Performance results collected on flights of five Arrow Mk. I aircraft fitted with Pratt & Whitney J-75 engines were used to estimate the performance of the Mk. II Arrow fitted with Iroquois engines. The Arrow with J-75 engines was heavier than with Iroquois and had to be ballasted for the correct centre of gravity position, Mk II with Iroquois engines did not need ballast and was about 5000 lbs lighter, and had 40 to 50% more thrust. It was estimated that [it] had a high chance of beating the world speed and altitude records held at that time by the United States." Given the controversy (and myths) now associated with the Arrow cancellation, it is perhaps revealing to compare basic details and performance capabilities of the Arrow Mk I and Mk II with much more contemporary aircraft.

Aircraft	Arrow Mk 1	Arrow Mk 2 (projected)	F-14 Tomcat	F-15 Eagle	Mig-25 Foxbat
First Flight	1958	n/a	1970	1972	1964
Length (feet)	80′ 10″	85′ 6″	62′ 8”	63′ 9″	78′ 2″
Wing Span (feet)	50′	50′	64′	42′ 10″	45′ 9″
Height (feet)	20′ 6″	21′	16′	18′6″	20′ 0″
Wing Area (ft^2)	1,225	1,225	565	608	612
Empty Weight (lbs)	49,040	45,000	40,104	28,600	44,100
Normal Weight (lbs)	57,000	62,431	58,715	44,630	-
Max Gross Wt (lbs)	68,602	68,847	74,348	56,000	82,500
Internal Fuel (Imp Gal)	2,897	3,297	2,865	2,486	3,830
Engines (ea 2)	P&W J-57	Iroquois	P&W TF30	P&W F100	Tumansky R-31
Thrust (lbs)	12,500	19,250	12,500	12,420	20,500
A/B Thrust(lbs)	18,500	26,000	20,900	23,830	27,000
Max Speed (40,000′)	M 2.0	M 2.0+	M 2.4	M 2.5	M 2.8
Combat Ceiling (ft)	53,000	58,500	50,000	63,000	75,460
Climb Rate (ft/min)	38,450	44,500	30,000	50,000	40,950
Combat Radius (mi)	300	408	765	-	460

In addition to the Mk II Arrow, there were projected development versions of the aircraft, including a Mk IIA version with increased internal fuel capacity and a Mk III version capable of MACH 3 performance.

FOLLOW-ON TESTING & RCAF BASING PLANS

The Arrow program was then unusual in that the program skipped over the prototype stage and moved directly instead to five pre-production aircraft. A further 29 Arrow Mk II aircraft were also in various stages on the production line at the time of the program cancellation.

Consequently, RCAF plans for follow-on testing and for the eventual service introduction were well developed. The first phase of testing by the company was to be followed by a preliminary RCAF evaluation also in Malton. After a period for checking of any modifications found necessary, the fourth phase was to consist of RCAF performance and handling trials. Next came an all-weather evaluation. The sixth phase was an intensive flying trials program followed by the aircraft weapons system evaluation in phase seven. Finally, operational suitability trials were to have confirmed the complete weapon system and would have developed maximum-effectiveness techniques for operational deployment.

Within the RCAF, the responsibility for the overall program testing, including phases 2, 4, 5 and 7, lay with the Central Experimental Proving Establishment (CEPE) located in Ottawa. However the majority of the testing, including phases 4, 5 and 7, was intended to be conducted using the CEPE facility at RCAF Station Cold Lake, Alberta. This station's main lodger unit was the Aircraft Armament Evaluation Detachment (AAED) of CEPE and it was in fact the first unit to be based at Cold Lake. It made use of a large weapons range area and a fully instrumented test range around Primrose Lake near the southern boundary of the range area. The other RCAF unit involved in the testing process was the Operational Proving Unit (OPU). This little-known unit was formed at RCAF Station Uplands. The OPU was to have been equipped with nine Arrow Mk II aircraft in addition to T-33, F-86 and CF-100 aircraft by the summer of 1962. Using these various aircraft, the OPU would have verified the operational suitability of the Arrow in simulated combat conditions. However, the unit formed and "then quietly stood down when the aircraft they were formed to operate, the Avro Arrow, was cancelled." CEPE and its AAED unit went on to become the Aerospace Engineering Test Establishment (AETE) still located today in Canadian Forces Base Cold Lake.

As part of the weapons testing phase, the Arrow aircraft would have fired missiles on the Primrose Test Range. Included in this phase were firings against live targets in the form of Ryan Firebee drones which would have been launched from Lancaster aircraft. The Firebee drones were acquired specifically for testing of the Sparrow II missiles for use on the CF-100 and CF-105 aircraft. In addition to the Lancaster aircraft, used as a launching platform and control mothership for the drones, H-34 helicopters were also stationed in Cold Lake to act as drone recovery aircraft.

What follows in the next section are the now-declassified plans for the RCAF's testing of the aircraft which include detailed references to each of the elements above.

References

AVRO Arrow. The Arrowheads, Boston Mills Press, Erin ON, Canada, 1980, ISBN 0-919822-35-5.

A History of the Air Defence of Canada 1948-1997. NBC Group, 71 Film Canada Inc, Ottawa ON, Canada, 1997.

Canadian Aircraft Since 1909. K.M. Molson & H.A. Taylor, Canada's Wings, Inc., Stittsville ON, Canada, 1982.

Janes All The World's Aircraft 1985–1986. Janes Publishing Company Ltd., London, England, 1985.

"Flying the Avro Arrow." Presentation to CASI Symposium, Jack Woodman, CASI Paper, 16 May 1978.

"Test Flying the Arrow (And Other High Speed Aircraft).", Jan Zurakowski, CAHS Journal, Winter 1979.

Appendix 1 to AVRO ARROW FLIGHT TEST SUMMARY

Avro Canada CF-105 Mk I Individual Aircraft Flight Records

(extract from: *Canadian Aircraft Since 1909* – K.M. Molson & H.A. Taylor, ISBN 0-920002-11-0)

Date	Flight No.	Duration (hr min)	Total (hr min)	Pilot	Purpose (and Remarks)
RCAF 25201					
25 Mar. 1958	1	35	35	Zurakowski	Initial flight. (Speeds up to 250 kt and altitude to 11,000 ft)
01 Apr. 1958	2	50	50	Zurakowski	(Nosewheel failed to retract. Flight restricted to handling below 250 kt. Altitude to 30,000 ft for cockpit pressurization check)
03 Apr. 1958	3	1 05	2 30	Zurakowski	M:1.1
15 Apr. 1958	4	1 15	3 45	Zurakowski	T.R.U. Unserviceable rendering telemetry inoperative. No high speed work
17 Apr. 1958	5	1 10	4 55	Zurakowski	Undercarriage snag after 'g' pull at 450 kt. Aborted high speed briefing
18 Apr. 1958	6	55	5 50	Zurakowski	M:1.25
18 Apr. 1958	7	40	6 30	Zurakowski	M:1.52 at 49,000 ft. Height of 50,000 ft reached
22 Apr. 1958	8	1 10	7 40	Woodman	Familiarization. M:1.4
23 Apr. 1958	9	45	8 25	Potocki	Familiarization. M:1.2
07 June 1958	10	1 45	10 10	Zurakowski	Damper troubles at take-off. Nose undercarriage door stuck down
11 June 1958	11	1 20	11 30	Zurakowski	Aircraft damaged on landing. Port gear lengthening mechanism unserviceable
05 Oct. 1958	12	1 20	12 50	Potocki	Acceptance (test) from production shop after repair. Subsonic
11 Dec. 1958	13	1 10	14 00	Potocki	Gear downmain door up check flight Modified elevator controls
15 Dec. 1958	14	1 25	15 25	Potocki	Damper checks restricted due to gear unsafe indication
20 Dec. 1958	15	1 25	16 50	Potocki	Continuation of damper checks. Speed restricted due to starboard gear not showing positive uplock. Pitch damper landing OK
21 Dec. 1958	16	45	17 35	Potocki	As per flight No. 15
05 Jan. 1959	17	1	18 35	Potocki	Damper system check. 20,000 ft
05 Jan. 1958	18	45	19 20	Potocki	Extension ASI to 650 kt at 17,000 ft
17 Jan. 1959	19	1	20 20	Potocki	Damper system checks and elevator hinge moment
24 Jan. 1959	20	1 5	21 25	Woodman	RCAF damper system check. Low level only due to weather
27 Jan. 1959	21	1	22 25	Potocki	General damper handling
31 Jan. 1959	22	45	23 10	Potocki	Extension of flight envelope
31 Jan. 1959	23	40	23 50	Potocki	Extension of flight envelope
07 Feb. 1959	24	1	24 50	Potocki	Climb stick tape. Roll and sideslip investigation up to M:1.3
19 Feb. 1959	25	50	25 40	Potocki	Stick tape and roll rates up to M:1.7
RCAF 25202					
01 Aug. 1958	1	1 35	1 35	Zurakowski	Initial flight. 30,000 ft
23 Aug. 1958	2	1	2 35	Zurakowski	M:1.5. Damper checks
26 Aug. 1958	3	1 5	3 40	Zurakowski	M:1.62
26 Aug. 1958	4	1	4 40	Zurakowski	M:1.7
27 Aug. 1958	5	1 5	5 45	Zurakowski	Ottawa telemetry check. M:1.5
28 Aug. 1958	6	1 5	6 50	Potocki	Damper handling M:1.7
28 Aug. 1958	7	1 20	8 10	Zurakowski	Ottawa telemetry check. M:1.72
14 Sep. 1958	8	1 5	9 15	Zurakowski	Damper handling. Telemetry unserviceable
14 Sep. 1958	9	1 10	10 25	Zurakowski	Damper checking. M:1.86 at 50,000 ft
16 Sep. 1958	10	1 10	11 35	Zurakowski	2.2 'g'. M:1.2 and damper check. Dutch roll investigation
26 Sep. 1958	11	1 5	12 40	Zurakowski	Pitch damper check. Subsonic
26 Sep. 1958	12	1	13 40	Zurakowski	M:1.55
28 Sep. 1958	13	55	14 35	Woodman	M:1.7 at 50,000 ft. RCAF handling
28 Sep. 1958	14	45	15 20	Potocki	M:1.55. 3 'g', 1.3 at 36,000 ft. Pitch oscillation +/- 3 'g'
03 Oct. 1958	15	1 25	16 45	Potocki	Pitch oscillation investigation
03 Oct. 1958	16	1 5	17 50	Cope	Familiarization. M:1.5
05 Oct. 1958	17	50	18 40	Potocki	All dampers up to M:1.45. 500 kt at 9,000 ft. Undercarriage doors open. Stick tape with yaw damper.
27 Oct. 1959	18	1 5	19 45	Potocki	Max speed 500 kt IAS at 7,500 ft on pivot door check. M:1.5 at 42,000 ft on damper checks. P/D not acceptable.
29 Oct. 1958	19	45	20 20	Potocki	Flutter check. M:1.7
29 Oct. 1959	20	45	21 15	Potocki	Flutter check. M:1.8
08 Nov. 1959	21	1 10	22 25	Potocki	Assessment of modified elevator. Parallel servo and feel trim to rear not satisfactory
11 Nov. 1959	22	1 15	23 40	Potocki	510 kt ASI 7,500 ft. Max speed of M:1.95 – 1.96 obtained from 50,000 ft Brake seizure on landing. Aircraft damaged. Starboard gear broken off.

Date	Flight No.	Duration (hr min)	Total (hr min)	Pilot	Purpose (and Remarks)
RCAF 25203					
22 Sep. 1958	1	1 35	1 35	Zurakowski	Initial flight. M:1.2
01 Oct. 1958	2	45	2 20	Potocki	Snag clearance. M:1.7
06 Oct. 1958	3	1	3 20	Cope	Performance 1A tailcones up to M:1.7 at 50,000 ft
16 Oct. 1958	4	1 10	4 30	Potocki	Fuel consumption and level speed checks at 35,000 ft. Subsonic
17 Oct. 1958	5	1 5	5 35	Woodman	Undercarriage door trouble starboard side. Low speed P.E.s with F86
18 Oct. 1958	6	1 10	6 45	Potocki	Level speeds and fuel consumption. Supersonic on climb
19 Oct. 1958	7	1 15	8 00	Woodman	Partial P.E.s, aborted high speed checks due to red light at M:0.95
31 Oct. 1958	8	1	9 00	Cope	Utility hydraulic failure. Gear down flight
07 Nov. 1958	9	1 10	10 10	Cope	Fuel consumption at 35,000 ft and single engine checks. Air conditioning failurerefrigerated. Subsonic
20 Jan. 1959	10	55	11 5	Potocki	Check flight to M:1.7 with modified elevator system. Aircraft turbine seized
01 Feb. 1959	11	1 15	12 20	Woodman	RCAF damper check
19 Feb. 1959	12	1 10	13 30	Potocki	Damper optimization. Observer D. E. Darrah carried.
RCAF 25204					
27 Oct. 1958	1	1 10	1 10	Potocki	Initial flight gear down 250 kt maximum
22 Nov. 1958	2	1 5	2 15	Potocki	Check flight
30 Nov. 1958	3	1 10	3 25	Potocki	Continuation of snag clearance to M:1.2
02 Feb. 1959	4	1 10	4 35	Cope	Check flight directed to Trenton
03 Feb. 1959	5	1 15	5 50	Potocki	Gear down ferry to base
07 Feb. 1959	6	1 10	7	Potocki	Clearance flight limited to M:1.5 by pedal judder
RCAF 25205					
11 Jan. 1958	1	40	40	Potocki	Initial flight gear down

Programme Terminated 20 February 1959

Extract of Arrow Annex & Appendices Prepared For 1957-58 RCAF Aircraft Procurement & Development Plans
(Note: Revised from original 8 1/2 X 14 format)

GLOSSARY OF ABBREVIATIONS

AAED	Aircraft Armament Evaluation Detachment (of CEPE)
ADC	Air Defence Command
ADAS	Airborne Data Acquisition System
AL	Amendment List
AMC	Air Material Command
AMCJS(W)	Air Material Command Joint Staff (Washington)
AST	Aircraft Systems Trainer
AW	All Weather
CEPE	Central Experimental Proving Establishment
CGI	Control Ground Intercept
CGTU	Conversion Ground Training Unit
ECM	Electronic Counter-Measures
GSE	Ground Support Equipment
IFF	Identification Friend or Foe
lbs	Pounds
nm	Nautical Miles
POL	Petrol Oil & Lubricants
OFTT	Operational Flight Tactics Trainer
OJT	On Job Training
OPU	Operational Proving Unit
OUT	Operational Training Unit
PMQ	Private Married Quarters
RCAF	Royal Canadian Air Force
SAGE	Semi-Automated Ground Environment
Sqn	Squadron
TACAN	TACtical Air Navigation system
UE	Unit Establishment
USAF	United States Air Force
WO	Warrant Officer
WPU	Weapons Proving Unit

TESTING & DEPLOYMENT SUMMARY

1   On 29 Oct 57 the Cabinet approved the continuation for another 12 months the development programme for the Arrow, including the ordering of 29 preproduction aircraft in addition to the eight already on order. The test and development trials started in Dec 57 and are scheduled for completion in Apr 61 when the first production aircraft is delivered to Air Defence Command (ADC). The initial tests will be carried out on the Arrow 1 followed by a complete evaluation programme for the Arrow 2.

2   The Arrow 1 is an interim test aircraft and differs from the Arrow 2 as follows:

	Arrow 1	Arrow 2
Engines	J-75	Iroquois
Astra	Interim Astra	Complete Astra
Armament	No armament Sparrow 2 pack to carry test instrumentation.	Four Sparrow 2 missiles in removable pack.
Power Supply	Compatible with Interim Astra.	Compatible with Interim Astra.
Air Conditioning	High pressure system dictated by the power plant.	Low pressure system dictated by the power plant.

3   The Arrow development schedule is composed of eight phases as follows:

(a)   **Phase 1:   Airworthiness Trials**
Contractor conducted ground and initial flight tests to determine airworthiness and to ensure that the aircraft with its installed and support equipment meets engineering specifications;

(b)   **Phase 2:   Contractor Compliance Trials**
RCAF tests to determine compliance with contractual requirements and to determine the performance and handling characteristics of the Arrow;

(c)   **Phase 3:   Design Requirements**
Contractor tests to overcome the deficiencies revealed in Phases 1 and 2;

(d)   **Phase 4:   Performance and Handling Trials**
RCAF tests to confirm the contractor's information and data on the performance and handling characteristic of the Arrow;

APPENDIX "C"

(e)   **Phase 5:   All-Weather Test**

RCAF test to obtain information on the characteristics, limitations and maintenance of the Arrow including installed equipment under adverse weather;

(f)   **Phase 6:   Intensive Flying**
RCAF trials on the aircraft and support equipment to reveal and correct any previously undetected design, functional and material defects;

(g)   **Phase 7:   Weapons Evaluations**
RCAF tests to evaluated the Arrow as a weapon with emphasis place on checking the effectiveness of the aircraft as a fighter rather than how it should be employed;

(h)   **Phase 8:   Operational Suitability Tests**
RCAF trials of tactically equipped aircraft and the support items to
determine their operational suitability.

4   **Programme Summary:**

Aircraft	Phase	Agency	Aircraft No.	Estimated Flying Hours
Arrow 1	1	AVRO	1, 2, 3, 4, 5 }	535
Arrow 1	2	CEPE	1, 2, 3 }	
Arrow 2	1	AVRO	6, 7, 8 }	254
Arrow 2	2	CEPE	6, 7, 8 }	
Arrow 2	3	AVRO	9, 10, 11, 12 13, 14, 15, 16	247
Arrow 2	4	CEPE	17, 18	150
Arrow 2	5	CEPE	19, 20	80
Arrow 2	Contractor Dev.	AVRO	21, 22	
Arrow 2	6	OPU	23, 24, 25	600
Arrow 2	7	CEPE	26, 27, 14, 15	450
Arrow 2	8	OPU	28, 29, 30, 31, 32, 33	650
Arrow 2	Attrition		34, 35, 36, 37	

About 3000 flying hours will be required to complete the test and evaluation of the Arrow.

The Arrow development schedule is as follows:

Date Trials Commence	Aircraft Assigned	Location	Type of Test
(a) Oct 58		Cold Lake	Sparrow 2 evaluation

(i)   Sparrow evaluation is scheduled to begin at Cold Lake Apr 59 with qualification of missiles to be completed by Mar 60 followed by development and demonstration of the Arrow weapons system.

(ii)   Four CF100 5M aircraft will be employed at Cold Lake on the Sparrow programme from Apr 59 until Mar 60. After Mar 60 two CF100 5M will be required for an indefinite period.

(iii)   KDA drones will be delivered to Cold Lake in Jun 58. Storage facilities are required.   See Annex 4.

(iv)   One H34 Helicopter is required for drone recovery by late 58.

(v)   The Cold Lake Evaluation System is required by early 59. See Annex 3 re status of the Evaluation System.

(i)   The two Lancaster 10DC aircraft of the Drone Flight will be located at Namao after Mar 60 to provide space at Cold Lake for Arrow trials.

(vii)   See Annex 1 regarding training requirement for Sparrow programme.

Date Trials Commence	Aircraft Assigned	Location	Type of Test
(b) Dec 57	1, 2, 3	Malton	Phase 1 Airworthiness

(i)   Contractor conducted ground and initial flight tests to determine airworthiness and to ensure that the Arrow 1 with its installed and supporting equipment meets engineering specifications. Flying to commence Mar 58.

(ii)   Maintenance Appraisal Teams have been assigned to AVRO, Canadair and RCA. The fourteen personnel engaged in this role will remain at the contractors until completion of the development programme. Then all or part of the MAT at AVRO may be used to assist with the Personnel Requirements Data study which is continuing.

(iii)   Three CEPE officers have been assigned to the AVRO Flight Test. These officers will probably accompany the contractor to Cold Lake in Mar 60 for the continuation of the Phase 3 trials.

APPENDIX "C"

Date Trials Commence	Aircraft Assigned	Location	Type of Test
(c) Jun 58	1, 2, 3	Malton	Phase 2 – Contractor compliance trials.

(i) CEPE tests to determine compliance with contractual requirments and to determine the performance and handling characteristics of the Arrow 1. This phase will also include a technical and functional evaluation of the installed and supporting equipment. The contractor will supply all support for RCAF Phase 2 testing.

(iii) Phases 1 and 2 will be, as far as possible, a CEPE/contractor integrated test programme and are scheduled to be completed by Jan 59.

(iii) The flying rate is estimated to be seven hours per aircraft per month.

Date Trials Commence	Aircraft Assigned	Location	Type of Test
(d) Nov 58	1, 2, 3	Malton	Phase 3 – Design Refinements

(i) Contractor conducted trials to overcome deficiencies revealed in Phases 1 and 2. These tests will be accomplished on the first three test aircraft and will continue until the Arrow 2 is available for Phase 3 trials approximately Dec 59.

(ii) The flying rate for Phase 3 is estimated to be seven hours per aircraft per month.

(iii) The three Arrow 1 aircraft used in Phases 1, 2 and 3 will require extensive modifications, installation of Astra and re-fitment with Iroquois engines before they an operational capability. The cost of such a modification programme, to provide limited operational capability, will preclude their assignment to ADC. These aircraft are scheduled to remain with the contractor for an indefinite period to meet further testing requirements.

Date Trials Commence	Aircraft Assigned	Location	Type of Test
(e) Sep 58	4, 5	Malton	Astra Development

(i) Astra flight development programme. The 4th and 5th Arrow 1 aircraft will be modified to carry the complete development Astra system. All the Astra components used will be hand built. Astra development tests are scheduled to be completed by the time the Arrow 2 is ready for Phase 3 trials approximately Dec 59.

(ii) Aircraft 4 and 5 will require refitment with production Astra and Iroquois engines as well as other modifications before they have a minimum operational capability. The cost of such a modification programme to provide limited capability will preclude their assignment to an operational role. These aircraft will be used by the contractor for an indefinite period to meet unforeseen additional testing required by the ancillary equipment.

Date Trials Commence	Aircraft Assigned		Location	Type of Test
(f) Mar 59	6, 7, 8 (Arrow 2)		Malton	Phase 1 – Airworthiness Trials
		(i)	Beginning of Arrow 2 trials. Phase 1 – contractor conducted ground and flight trials to determine airworthiness and to ensure that the Arrow 2 with its installed and supporting equipment meets engineering specifications.	
(g) Jun 59	6, 7, 8		Malton	Phase 2 – Contractor compliance trials

    (i)   Phase 2 – Conducted by CEPE to determine compliance with contractual requirements and to determine handling and performance characteristics. These three aircraft will <u>not</u> be fully equipped with ASTRA. As far as possible, Phases 1 and 2 will be a CEPE/contractor integrated test programme. Support for CEPE Phase 2 trials will be supplied by the contractor, RCAF testing is scheduled for completion Jan 60. The flying rate is estimated to be seven hours per aircraft per month.

    (ii)   These three aircraft will require fitment with ASTRA as well as extensive modifications before they have an operational capability. They will remain with the contractor for an in-definite period to assist with Phase 3 continuation trials and other tests.

    (iii)   The first eight Arrow development aircraft have been programmed to remain at Malton with the contractor for an indefinite period as past experience has shown that test aircraft are required at the contractor to meet continuing development trials.

    (iv)   Training of RCAF servicing personnel must start at the contractor operated school in Jun 59 the same time Arrow 2 Date Phase 2 commences. Between Jun 59 and Jun 60 the contractor will train selected CEPE and certain AMC and ADC staff personnel. As nine months is required to train a limited number of technicians on certain aspects of the ASTRA, some training must start in Dec 59 to have CEPE personnel available to support Phase 5 aircraft flown to Cold Lake in Aug 60.

    (v)   An Aircraft Systems Trainer will be required by Jan 60 at the Arrow Conversion Ground Training Unit, Camp Borden.

    (vi)   See Annex 1 regarding RCAF Arrow Training Programme.

APPENDIX "C"

Date Trials Commence	Aircraft Assigned		Location	Type of Test
(h) Dec 59	9, 10, 11, 12 13, 14, 15, 16		Malton	Phase 3 – Design Refinement

	(i)	Contractor conducted trials to overcome deficiencies revealed in Phases 1 and 2. Seven aircraft have been allotted to Phase 3. All aircraft will be equipped with pre-production ASTRA with the exception of No. 11, which will be used for special engine and airframe tests. No. 16 will be used by the contractor at Malton on structural integrity tests.

20, 21	(i)	Aircraft 20, 21 will be used by the contractor at Malton on further contractor development trials.

Date Trials Commence	Aircraft Assigned		Location	Type of Test
(j) Mar 60	11, 12, 13		Cold Lake	Continuation of Phase 3 and Demonstration of Weapon System

	(i)	After three months testing at Malton five of the seven aircraft will be flown to Cold Lake beginning in Mar 60 to continue Phase 3.
	(ii)	Staging facilities will be required by the contractor by Mar 60 and for the RCAF by Jul 60. Although the contractor will be responsible for flying the four aircraft to Cold Lake the RCAF will assist with the staging.
	(iii)	See Annex 2 regarding Arrow Staging Facilities.
	(iv)	In so far as missile instrumentation is concerned, the Cold Lake range facilities required by Apr 59 for Sparrow II trials will be satisfactory for both Phase 3 and 7 Arrow 2 trials additional test instrumentation is required to cater to Arrow 2 testing.
	(v)	See Annex 3 regarding Cold Lake Evaluation System for Sparrow and Arrow Trials.
	(vi)	Commencing Mar 60 the contractor will require personnel accommodation on a continuing and transient basis and also hangar facilities.
	(vii)	See Annex 4 regarding Cold Lake Hangar and Other Accommodation Requirements.
	(viii)	Phase 3 trials at Cold Lake conclude with the contractor demonstrating to the RCAF that the Arrow Weapon System meets RCAF specifications, Phase 3 is scheduled for completion about Mar 61, however the weapon system demonstration will continue until Mar 62. Aircraft 12 and 13 will be used for the Weapon System demonstration and aircraft 14 and 15 will be assigned to Phase 7 in Apr 61.

Date Trials Commence	Aircraft Assigned	Location	Type of Test
(k) Jul 60	17, 18	Cold Lake	Phase 4 – Performance & Handling Trials

(i) Beginning of the RCAF Arrow 2 evaluation programme.

(ii) Phase 4, CEPE tests to confirm the contractor's information and data on the performance and handling characteristics of the Arrow 2. Phase 4 is scheduled to be completed by May 61.

(iii) Preliminary Engineering Orders prepared by the contractor, must be available when these trials commence.

(iv) Aircraft 17 and 18 will not be equipped with ASTRA for these Trials. The two aircraft will be flown to Cold Lake by CEPE in Jul 60.

(v) Phase 4 trials must be conducted on the first production aircraft unless it can be assured that the preproduction aircraft have the same performance and handling characteristics.

(vi) The performance and handling data provided by the contractor and confirmed by the RCAF during Phase 4 will be used to compile pilots operating instructions which must be available before the Arrow is introduced in Sqn service Apr 61. Preliminary pilots operating instructions are required in Sep 60 when Phase 6 begins.

(vii) The flying rate for Phase 4 is nine per aircraft per month.

Date Trials Commence	Aircraft Assigned	Location	Type of Test
(l) Aug 60	19, 20	Cold Lake	Phase 5 – All Weather Test

(i) CEPE tests to obtain information on the characteristics, limitations and maintenance of the Arrow 2 including installed equipment under adverse weather conditions.

(ii) Aircraft 19 and 20, fully operational, will be flown to Cold Lake by the RCAF in Aug 60. CEPE will conduct Phase 5 which is scheduled for completion Apr 61. Additional all-weather testing, if necessary, will be conducted during the winter of 61-62, on aircraft 14 and 15, assigned to Phase 7 Apr 61.

(iii) Personnel fully qualified in ASTRA maintenance must be available by Aug 60. See Annex 1.

APPENDIX "C"

Date Trials Commence	Aircraft Assigned	Location	Type of Test
(m) Sep 60	23, 24, 25	Uplands	Phase 6 – Intensive Flying

(i)	RCAF trials on the aircraft and support equipment to reveal and correct any previously undetected design, functional and material defects.
(ii)	Phase 6 will be conducted at Uplands as hangar accommodation is not available at Cold Lake.
(iii)	See Annex 5 regarding Base for Phase 6 and 8 Trials.
(iv)	The OPU with CEPE assistance will carry out Phase 6 testing. The three aircraft tentatively assigned to the trials will not be fully equipped with ASTRA. The flying rate for Phase 6 is 25 hours per aircraft per month.
(v)	Phase 6 is scheduled for completion Apr 61.
(vi)	An Aircraft Systems Trainer and an Operational Flight and Tactics Trainer are required by Jun 60 for aircrew conversion training.
(vii)	Sufficient ADC aircrew and servicing personnel must be available by Sep 60 to support Phase 6 trials. See Annex 1 regarding Arrow Training Programme.
(viii)	Engineering Orders must be available when Phase 6 commences.

Date Trials Commence	Aircraft Assigned	Location	Type of Test
(n) Jan 61	26, 27	Cold Lake	Phase 7- Weapons Evaluation
Apr 61	14, 15		

(i)	Phase 7, CEPE/AAED trials to evaluate the Arrow 2 as a weapon with emphasis on the effectiveness of the aircraft as fighter. This Phase is an extension of the contractor's weapon system demonstration.
(ii)	Aircraft 26 and 27 will be fully operational. In Apr 61 aircraft 14 and 15 will be assigned to Phase 7. Although Phase 7 will continue for an indefinite period, after Sep 62 only two aircraft will be used as 14 and 15 will be assigned to ADC. The flying rate for this test is 25 hours per aircraft per month.
(iii)	Two CF100 ECM equipped aircraft will be required in Jan 61 for Phase 7.

Date Trials Commence	Aircraft Assigned	Location	Type of Test
(o) Feb 61 31, 32, 33	28, 29, 30,	Uplands	Phase 8 – Operational Suitability Test

(i)	The OPU, with CEPE assistance if required, will conduct Phase 8 at Uplands, the same base as Phase 6. Phase 8 must be conducted with the SAGE environment. See Annex 5 regarding Base for Phases 6 and 8. Six fully operational Arrow 2 aircraft are tentatively scheduled for this test.

Date Trials Commence	Aircraft Assigned		Location	Type of Test
		(ii)	By Feb 61 sufficient ADC aircrew and servicing personnel must be trained to support the twelve aircraft assigned to Phases 6 & 8.	
		(iii)	On completion of Phase 8 in Jul 61 three of the test aircraft will be assigned to ADC operations and three will remain with the OPU for continuation of operational testing. The flying rate is 25 hours per aircraft per month.	
	34, 35 36, 37			Attrition
		(i)	During the eight test phases four aircraft have been allocated to meet any attrition. Approximately 3000 flying hours will be required to complete the Arrow development programme.	
(p) Apr 61			Arrow Conversion Unit or first ADC Sqn to be equipped with Arrow 2	ADC Operations
		(i)	First operational Arrow 2 delivered to ADC. Because of the nature of the development programme all results of the trials will not have been incorporated in production aircraft by the time the first aircraft are delivered to ADC. Hence the first operational aircraft may not necessarily meet the OCH. However, their capability will have been established and as the results of the RCAF evaluation programme become available early production aircraft will be modified to meet the OCH.	
(q) May 61	19, 20			ADC Operations
		(i)	On completion of Phase 5 – All-Weather Trials, conducted during the winter of 60-61, aircraft 19 and 20 will be delivered to ADC in May 61.	
		(ii)	Further All-Weather testing, if necessary, will be conducted on aircraft assigned to Phase 7 which is expected to continue for an indefinite period.	
(r) Jul 61	31, 32, 33			ADC Operations
		(i)	On completion of Phase 8 three of the six test aircraft will be delivered to ADC about Sep 61. Aircraft 28, 29 and 30 will remain with the OPU for continuation of operational testing.	

APPENDIX "C"

Date Trials Commence	Aircraft Assigned		Location	Type of Test
(s) Apr 62	17, 18			ADC Operations
		(i)	After being modified and equipped with ASTRA these two aircraft, which were used in Phase 4, will be delivered to ADC in Apr 62, Phase 4 is scheduled for completion by Apr 61 and about one year will be required to complete modifications and install ASTRA.	
(t) Apr 62	23, 24, 25			ADC Operations
		(i)	The three aircraft used in Phase 6, which concludes Apr 61, will be delivered to ADC about Apr 62 after being equipped with ASTRA and modified as required by the results of other trials. The modification programme will take about one year.	
(u) Sep 62	9, 10, 11			ADC Operations
		(i)	These three aircraft used by the contractor at Malton for Phase 3 trials will be assigned to ADC about Sep 62 after being modified to bring them up to the required operational standard. No. 11 aircraft will require ASTRA fitment.	
		(ii)	After Sep 62 Phase 3 continuation trials, if required, will be conducted on aircraft one to eight and No. 16 which will remain with the contractor for an indefinite period.	
(v) Jan 63	14, 15			ADC Operations
		(i)	Aircraft 14 and 15 used in Phases 3 and 7 trials will be assigned to ADC about Jan 63 after being modified to bring them up to the required operational standard. Aircraft 26 and 27 also used on Phase 7 will remain with CEPE/AAED for an indefinite period to meet further testing requirements.	
(w) Mar 63	12, 13, 21, 22			ADC Operations
		(i)	Aircraft 12 and 13 used by the contractor on the continuation of Phase 3 – Weapon System demonstration at Cold Lake will be assigned to ADC about Mar 63 after being modified to bring them up to the required operational standard.	

The build-up of the Arrow UEs to 12 aircraft per squadron shown in the ADC Section of the programme is based on a production rate of four Arrow aircraft per month commencing in Apr 61.

RCAF ARROW TRAINING PROGRAMME

1.   The introduction of the Arrow has raised the requirement for a training programme which, because of the complexity of the aircraft systems and the large number of aircraft involved, will be larger and more extensive than ever before required when introducing a new aircraft. For example, CEPE will need about 300 personnel trained in all aspects of Arrow maintenance by mid-1960 and the OPU will need 400 fully trained personnel by the end of 1960 to support Phases 6 and 8. The training of squadron maintenance personnel should also start in 1960. Therefore, between commencement of ground training, which should start in Jun 59, and conversion of the first sqn in Apr 61, about 110 personnel must be trained. A large instructional staff will be needed. In addition an aircrew conversion programme is required. The length of ground training course will vary between eight weeks and nine months.

Training Requirement

2.   In general terms the training required to support the introduction of the 37 Arrow aircraft is outlined as follows:

Type of Training	DURATION	No of Trainees	TIMING	REMARKS
1. Sparrow	16 wks	19 all ranks	The 2nd of two courses was completed during the spring 1958	(a) Courses arranged through USN (b) Three officers and eight technicians to be assigned to the Sparrow evaluation programme and Arrow Phases 3 & 7 trials
	16 wks	6 all ranks	Training to be completed by early 1960.	(a) A minimum of sic technicians to be trained as CGTU Sparrow instructors by early 1960.
2. Drone Servicing	2 mos	2 Officers 23 Technicians	Training to be completed by 1 Oct 58	(a) Arrangements are being made with the contractor to train these personnel. (b) This establishment should be increased to about 50 when the Arrow programme starts. Training on high speed drones will be required.

ANNEX 1 TO
APPENDIX "C"
To Programme of Activities
1958–1962

Type of Training	DURATION	No of Trainees	TIMING	REMARKS
3. Maintenance & Operations of Cold Lake Range Facilities.	10-12 wks	5 Officers 27 Technicians	Training to be completed by Apr 59 (OJT).	(a) Range personnel are required for Sparrow 2 trials. It is expected that this establishment will meet Arrow evaluation requirements.
4. Telemetering equipment for Sparrow.	10-12 weeks	12 Technicians	Training to be completed by Apr 59 (OJT).	(a) These technicians, assigned to the Airborne Laboratory, are required to checkout the telemetering equipment for Sparrow 2.
5. Airborne Data Acquisition System.	10-12 weeks	13 Technicians	Training to be completed by Mar 60.	(a) In Mar 60, the staff of the Airborne Instrumentation Laboratory to increased by 13 technicians to maintain the Airborne Data Acquisition System installed in Arrow test aircraft.
6. Arrow CGTU Staff.		(Approx 80)	Instructors to be available to TC starting 1 Jan 59.	(a) Instructors will be needed in late 1959 to staff the Arrow conversion ground training unit. This unit will be required to train about 300 CEPE personnel by early 1960, 400 ADC personnel by late 1960 for Phases 6 and 8 and ADC personnel to support the Arrow sqn conversion programme by early 1961. The trainee population at the Arrow Conversion Ground Training Unit will average about 300 during 1960, 61 and part of 62.

Type of Training	DURATION	No of Trainees	TIMING	REMARKS
7. Arrow Electronic Systems Training:		A total of 12 officers and 138 technicians is required to support the CEPE Arrow evaluation programme. Below is a breakdown of the number of personnel taking the various courses.	Of the total of 12 officers and 138 technicians, the training of 4 officers and 46 technicians to be completed by Mar 60 to support Phase 3; the remaining 8 officers and 92 technicians should be trained by Sep 60 to support Phases 7 & 8.	RCA is providing a training programme which will include layouts for AES sub-system training benches in an attempt to meet AST requirements.
(a) Air Data, Navigation, Platform and Automatic Flight Control Systems.	6 mons	3 Officers 47 Technicians		
(b) Fire Control System	6 mons	3 Officers 44 Technicians		
(c) IFF L&S Band Homers Doppler, TACAN	3 mons	3 Officers 14 Technicians		
(d) Airborne I/C A/G Communications, Data Link	3 mons	3 Officers 33 Technicians		
(e) Complete Electronic System	3 mons	12 Officers 27 Technicians		All the 12 officers and 27 technicians selected from the Arrow Electronic Systems courses outlined in 7(a)(b)(c)(d) to take this training.
8. Arrow 2 Engine, Airframe GSE maintenance	8-12 weeks	(a) 60 all ranks (approx)	Training to be completed by Mar 60.	(a) Required by CEPE to support contractor's Phase 3 continuation trials at Cold Lake.
		(b) 120 all ranks (approx)	Training to be completed by Jul 60.	(a) About 120 technicians in addition to the 60 technicians already supporting Arrow trials at Cold Lake and shown above, will be required by CEPE for Phases 4,5 and 7.
9. Arrow 2 maintenance (all aspects)	8-12 weeks	400 all ranks (approx)	All training except Astra to be completed by Feb 61	(a) About 400 personnel will be required by the OPU to conduct Phases 6 & 8.

ANNEX 1 TO
APPENDIX "C"
To Programme of Activities
1958–1962

Type of Training	DURATION	No of Trainees	TIMING	REMARKS
				(b) The number of personnel needed to support Arrow 2 maintenance exclusive of Astra will not be known until about Jul 58 when the Personnel Requirements Data Study is completed at AVRO.
Aircrew Training				
(a) CEPE		3		(a) Two pilots and one observer have already been selected by CEPE. CEPE aircrew will be trained by the contractor.
(a) OPU	not known	12 Pilots 6 Observers (AI)	Six pilots required by Sep 60. Six pilots and six observers required by Feb 61.	(a) Aircrew suitable for employment on Phases 6 and 8 should be selected by ADC and assigned to the OPU in sufficient time to be trained before the trials commence. Selected crews should be assigned to CEPE in early 60 for Arrow familiarization and training. The requirement for test pilot course and training on delta aircraft should be investigated and if necessary the crews should receive this training before being assigned to the OPU

Training Facilities

3   Present plans call for the initial Arrow training of service personnel to be provided by the contractors, a limited number of CEPE and certain AMC and ADC staff personnel will be trained by the Contractor between 1 Jun 59 and Jan 60. Commencing in Jan 60 sufficient maintenance personnel will be trained to accept the first five aircraft and to provide and instructional cadre for the Arrow CGTU. Arrow training can best be accomplished if all ground training is concentrated at one base and under the

supervision of one OC. This facility, which initially will be operated by the contractor will be located at RCAF Stn Camp Borden where facilities can be made available and the transition of the school to service operation can take place without interrupting training. Preliminary studies indicated that about 25,000-30,000 sq ft of floor space is required by the Arrow Conversion Ground Training Unit.

Responsibility for Arrow Ground Training

4   Training Command has been given the responsibility of Arrow maintenance trades training. The Arrow Conversion Ground Training Unit is to be ready to commence training at Camp Borden at 1 Jan 60.

Aircrew Training

5   CEPE aircrew for the Arrow evaluation have already been selected and a training programme is underway. Early in 1958 ADC should select aircrew for assignment to Phases 6 and 8 and the details of an aircrew training programme worked out.

6   On the basis that Phases 6 and 8 will be conducted at Uplands consideration should given to locating the aircrew training facility there also. Space for an Aircraft Systems Trainer and an Operational Flight Tactics Trainer will be required.

Synthetic Trainers

7   AIRCRAFT SYSTEMS TRAINERS: Two AST's are needed to support technician and aircrew training as follows:

(a) 1st AST: The 1st AST is now in development and should be in operation by Jan 60. This AST will be used at the Arrow Conversion Ground Training Unit , Camp Borden, for all Arrow aircraft technician training.

(b) 2nd AST: This AST built to configuration of the 18th Arrow, will be needed for aircraft conversion training.

8   ASTRA TRAINERS. It is estimated that 300 to 400 of the 1100 tradesmen required by Apr 61 will need varying degrees of training on the Astra integrated flight system. This will produce an average trainee population of about 100 students at the Arrow training facility. RCA is providing an Astra training programme, and indications are that the lengths of the courses will vary from three to nine months. Although only one Astra system has been allotted to training, the components of three systems are required to meet the training programme. A complete Astra system trainer will need about 8000 square feet of floor space.

9   OPERATIONAL FLIGHT AND TACTICS TRAINER. Because no dual Arrow aircraft are being considered there is an urgent requirement for OFTTs. The first OFTT will be needed at Uplands in Sep 60 to support ADC aircrew training for Phases 6 and 8. On completion of the initial conversion training programme this trainer will be assigned either to the Arrow OTU or will remain at Uplands for sqn continuation training. This OFTT should be ordered by mid-1958.

ANNEX 2
To APPENDIX "C"
To Programme of Activities
1958–1962

ARROW STAGING FACILITIES

1   Staging facilities will be required by the contractor in Mar 60 and the RCAF in Jul 60 as is will not be practical to fly test Arrow aircraft from Malton to Cold Lake non-stop. The ferrying range of the Arrow is about 1400 nm and the direct route between Toronto and Cold Lake is 1350 nm. Although the contractor will be responsible for flying the four aircraft for Phase 3 continuation trials the RCAF will assist with the staging.

Staging Requirement

2   (a)   STAGING BASE LOCATION: The staging base should be located about 60-70% of the distance between Toronto and Cold Lake.

(b)   RUNWAY: The minimum runway requirements for ferrying development Arrow aircraft are 10,000 feet long (sea level conditions) and 200 feet wide to support a maximum gross weight of 70,000 lbs with a bearing pressure of 260 lbs psi. The minimum runway length requirement for operational Arrow aircraft is 8,000 feet with two 1000 ft overshoot areas.

(c)   POL: There are no special POL requirements. Only normal RCAF spec POL for jet aircraft will be required.

(d)   SERVICING REQUIREMENT: In addition to normal servicing equipment, the following equipment peculiar to the Arrow will be required:

(i)   Air Conditioning unit,

(ii)   Power Unit,

(iii)   Starting Unit,

(iv)   Liquid oxygen replenishing facilities.

(e)   PERSONNEL: A crew of one WO and about ten technicians will be required to service an Arrow at the staging base.

Frequency of Use

3   The staging base will be used about once a month for approximately ten months beginning Mar 60 for ferrying Arrow test aircraft to Cold Lake. Additional flights may be required if it is necessary for these aircraft to return to Malton for factory modifications or maintenance. Should an Arrow OTU be established at Cold Lake the requirement for a staging facility would continue.

Review of Suitably Located Bases

4   The Canadian airfields that most nearly meet operational requirements and are located with the desirable staging range are as follows:

DEPARTMENT OF TRANSPORT

	Runway Length	Gross WT Capacity	Dist From Toronto
Regina	6,400	90,000 lbs	1,098 nm
Saskatoon	8,300	62,000 lbs	1,200 nm
Winnipeg	7,000	150,000 lbs	812 nm

RCAF

	Runway Length	Gross WT Capacity	Dist From Toronto
Gimli	7,200	30,000 lbs	822 nm
Portage la Prairie	7,000	70,000 lbs	850 nm
MacDonald	7,000	86,000 lbs	862 nm

Based on the minimum operational requirements outlined in para 2 above it is apparent that there are no suitable staging facilities already available in Canada.

5   US Base. Headquarters USAF has concurred in an RCAF request for the use of the USAF base at Minot North Dakota area for staging Arrow aircraft during the test period. Headquarters USAF has authorized direct communications between AMCJS(W) and USAF ADC for the detailed planning of the staging.

ANNEX 3
To APPENDIX "C"
To Programme of Activities
1958–1962

COLD LAKE EVALUATION SYSTEM
FOR
SPARROW AND ARROW TRIALS

Basic System

1   The evaluation system required for the Sparrow 2 and Arrow evaluation programme is composed of a Data Collecting and Processing Unit, a check-out facility for airborne equipment and an airborne Data Acquisition System in the Arrow. Because of the distance separating Cold Lake Station from the range site the Data Collecting and Processing unit is divided into two components; a Data Collection Facility at the range and a Data Processing Facility at Cold Lake Station. Data collected at the range is converted to digital form and transmitted over a radio link to the Data Processing Facility at Cold Lake Station. Information gathered during the flight will be either telemetered to the Data Collection Facility or recorded on magnetic tapes and film strips which form part of the Airborne Data Acquisition System installed in all Arrow test aircraft. A Check-out Facility will be use to pre-flight check airborne test equipment.

Cold Lake Range Data Collection Facility.

2   The Data Collection Facility is composed of the following units:

(a)   PRIMARY DATA COLLECTION SYSTEM: This system receives and records on magnetic tape, FM/FM, PDM/FM or PDM/FM/FM type of telemetered signals. Concurrently with the recording of data on magnetic tape, these data are fed to the appropriate ground station during real-time operation for the production of Quick-look real-time records. The system should be capable of playing back, after completion of a specified test, the magnetic tapes to the appropriate ground station for further processing. Duplicate installation of antennas, receivers, recorders, etc. are required to provide and operational back-up.

(b)   FM GROUND STATION: This station accepts the complex FM signal, either directly from the FM receivers at real-time rates or from the magnetic tapes during play-back. The system should be capable of accepting any 12 of the 18 standard sub-carrier frequencies as laid down by the Inter-Range Instrumentation Group, including the capability for accepting the top five frequencies with frequency deviation of ± 15%.

(c)   PDM GROUND STATION: This station accepts PDM data, either directly from the PDM receivers at real-time rates or from the magnetic tapes during play-back.

(d)   QUICK-LOOK RECORDING SYSTEM: This system contains two independent recorders capable of recording simultaneously at least 16 channels of data of data form d.c. up a data frequency of 2 kcs.

(e)   PULSE CODETELEMETERING SYSTEM: This system accepts data from the FM and/or PDM Ground Stations and converts it into digital code for transmission over the radio link to the Cold Lake Station Data Processing Facility.

Radio Link

3   Data compiled at the Cold Lake Range Data Collection Facility is transmitted to the Data Processing Facility at Cold Lake station over a line-of-sight range of about 30 miles. This radio link should operate either on the 216 to 245 mcs or the 800 to 850 mcs frequency range.

Kinetheodolites

4   Nine kinetheodolites are located at the Cold Lake Range. An investigation is underway to determine the possibility of automatically reducing data from the theodolites without unacceptable losses in accuracy. In addition, an investigation is required to determine whether the maximum speed and altitude capabilities of the present kinetheodolites meet Arrow and Sparrow 2 requirements.

Cold Lake Station Data Processing Facility

5   The Data Processing Facility is composed of the following units:

(a)   PCM DATA COLLECTION SYSTEM. This system accepts the digital code, as transmitted over the radio link from the range, through a receiver and converts these data to a parallel code suitable for recording on a digital magnetic tape recorder.

(b)   QUICK-LOOK RECORDING. A Quick-look recording system capable of recording (for editing purposes) data in the form of at least six selected simultaneous analog traces is required.

(c)   DATA PROCESSING FOR COMPUTER: The Data Processor converts data to a format suitable for an IBM computer. The system contains a Programme and Control feature enabling selection of data to be translated onto computer tape. In addition a computer of the IBM 704 type together with plotting and printing equipment is required for Arrow evaluation.

(d)   TEST AND CALIBRATION EQUIPMENT: Special test and calibration equipment for the routine operation and maintenance of the complete Data Processing Facility is required.

Airborne Data Acquisition System

6   Most of the evaluation data gathered during flight will be recorded on magnetic tapes and film strips of the Airborne Data Acquisition System which will be installed in all Arrow aircraft at Cold Lake. This equipment must be available by early 1960.

Magnetic Tape Recorder/Reproducer Equipment

7   A 14-track magnetic tape recorder/reproducer is required at Cold Lake Station to record the data collected by the Airborne Acquisition System installed in the Arrow. However, to process data for reduction the following additional equipment is required:

ANNEX 3
To APPENDIX "C"
To Programme of Activities
1958–1962

- - -

    (a)   Discrimators, selector units and filters, as well as,

    (b)   PDM decommutator and associated equipment.

Check-out Facility

8   A PDM and FM monitoring system is required to check-out the airborne test equipment at Cold Lake Station. This facility should record at least six traces of PDM data or four traces of FM data simultaneously.

9   By Mar 60 the capacity of the check-out facility must be increased to 45 traces of PDM and 14 traces of FM to handle both Arrow and Sparrow 2 testing.

Data Link - Ground Environment

10   A AN/GKA-5 Data Link ground station to test the operational modes of the Arrow Weapons System has been ordered and delivery is expected in Aug 58. Tentative planning calls for this equipment to be set up initially at RCA Camden; then at Malton for initial Arrow trials; and move to Cold Lake Mar 60 for Arrow continuation testing.

Precision Radar

11   The three M33-C AA radars, already in operation at the Cold lake Range will be required for the Sparrow 2 evaluation programme. An investigation of the capabilities of these radars should be made to determine the operating limits and if any modifications are required for the Arrow evaluation programme.

CGI

12   The Arrow evaluation programme will require complete CGI coverage to at least 200 miles and altitudes up to 70,000 feet. Modifications to improve range and height are planned for the present CGI. These are scheduled to be completed before Mar 60 when the Arrow evaluation programme begins at Cold Lake. These improvements will meet the Arrow evaluation programme requirements.

Construction Requirements

13   See Annex 4 - Cold Lake - Hangar and Other Accommodation Requirements

Personnel Requirements

14   COLD LAKE RANGE FACILITIES: The personnel establishment required to operate the Range Facilities during the Sparrow 2 evaluation programme is five officers and 27 other ranks. It is anticipated that this establishment will meet Arrow requirements. Range personnel are required by Apr 59 for the Sparrow programme, however, the date set for transferring these people to Cold Lake should be governed by the comments in para 16 below.

15   **Cold Lake Station:**

(a)   AIRBORNE INSTRUMENTATION LABORATORY: Twelve personnel are required to check-out the telemetering equipment for the Sparrow 2. These technicians are required by Apr 59.

(b)   In Mar 60 the establishment in 15(a) above should be increased to about 25 to include personnel to maintain the Airborne Data Acquisition System.

(c)   DATA PROCESSING FACILITY: The Data Facility will be operated under a civilian contract. The agreement calls for the contractor to operate and maintain existing processing equipment as well as the additional equipment required for Arrow 2 and Arrow programmes. Although the number of personnel required will vary because of fluctuations in workload it is expected that on the average about 25 civilians will be required at Cold Lake throughout the Sparrow 2 and Arrow evaluation programmes.

Status of Evaluation System

16   Assuming that the contract for the ground telemetry and data processing system was let by May 58 eight months will be required to install and check-out the system. The evaluation system will be operational about 01 Jan 59, in time to meet the commencement of Sparrow 2 trials scheduled for Apr 59.

ANNEX 4
To APPENDIX "C"
To Programme of Activities
1958–1962

COLD LAKE HANGAR
AND OTHER ACCOMMODATION REQUIREMENTS

Hangar Accommodation Requirements

1 During the period in question indications are that the following aircraft will be established at the units indicated:

			58-59	59-60	60-61	61-62
(a)	3(AW) OTU	CF100	62	62	62	62
		T33	2	2	2	2
		Dakota	2	2	2	2
(b)	Weapons Training Unit	CF100	3	3	3	3
		T33	8	8	8	8
		CF100 (Visiting Sqn)	9	9	9	9
(c)	Cold Lake Station	Dakota 4or4M	1	1	1	1
		H5	1	1	1	1
		Otter	1	1	1	1
(d)	AAED	T33	1			
		Mitchell 1				
		Lanc 10DC	2	2	(based at Namao after Mar 60)	
		F86 (chase and tow a/c)	3	3	2	2
		H34	1	1	1	1
		CF100 (chase a/c)	3	7	7	4
		CF100 5M	6	6	4	2
		CF100 4A (ECM a/c)	1	1	2	-
		Arrow		4	10	8

2   Assuming adequate first line maintenance conditions for all aircraft and 100 percent coverage for the Arrow aircraft employed on Phases 3, 4, 5 and 7 the following steel arch hangars are required:

	58-59	59-60	60-61	61-62
CF100, duals 4A, 5M	6.7	6.7	6.8	6.7
T33, Otter, F86, Mitchell, H5,H34 Lanc 10DC	1.5	1.5	1.3	1.3
Arrow	-	0.7 Mar60	1.3 Jul60 1.7 Jan61	1.7
	8.2	8.9	9.8	9.7

There are only one Stage II Cantilever and five Steel Arch hangars at Cold Lake. On the assumption that the Stage II Cantilever is equivalent to 2.5 steel arch hangars, the following additional hangars are required:

	58-59	59-60	60-61	61-62
Additional Steel Arch Hangars Required	0.7	1.4	2.3	2.2

3   Based on the aircraft establishments outlined in para (1) the Cold Lake units should be able to cope during 1958-59 by accepting hangar allotments slightly below the approved minimum requirements. However CEPE has stated that the hangar space available to AAED is not adequate for present commitments and that the situation will be worse in 1958-59 when the Argus is tested. Therefore, Mar 60 when the Arrow trials begin, the hangar deficiency becomes critical. The requirement for additional hangars would be difficult to support because of the short term nature of the evaluation programme. Moreover, even if approval for the hangars were sought immediately, construction would not be completed in time. Therefore the only alternative action is to remove or cut-back some the Cold Lake units during the 1960 to 62 critical period.

4   CEPE/AAED HANGAR REQUIREMENT. Mar 60 to late 62 CEPE/AAED hangar requirements, in addition to the steel arch hangar already occupied are as follows:

(a)   One Stage II Centilever or,
(b)   One Steel Arch and 0.5 Stage II Cantilever or,
(c)   Two steel arch hangars.

This hangarage will accommodate the AAED aircraft shown in para 1 (d) and the Cold Lake station aircraft shown in para 1 (c) which, with the exception of the Expeditors, are required for search and rescue and range operation. Although it would be desirable to have all Arrow maintenance consolidated in the

ANNEX 4
To APPENDIX "C"
To Programme of Activities
1958–1962

Stage II cantilever and the chase, etc aircraft accommodated in the AAED steel arch hangar this may not be practical when all factors are considered. For instance central maintenance and CF100 facilities are located in this hangar. These would have to be relocated if the cantilever were modified to accommodate the Arrow. It may therefore be more practical and economical to modify a steel arch hangar for the Arrow trials than relocate central maintenance. Feasibility/cost studies on modifying steel arch and cantilever hangars for the Arrow evaluation are being carried out.

5   POSSIBLE COURSE OF ACTION TO PROVIDE HANGAR ACCOMMODATION FOR ARROWEVALUATION. Assuming that no additional hangars will be constructed to provide the necessary accommodation, the following action would provide the space required:

      (a)   REDUCE 3 (AW) OTU AIRCRAFT UE AND STAND-DOWN THE WPU DURING THE WINTER. Accommodation equivalent to one steel arch hangar can be made available by standing down the WPU during the two critical winter periods of 60-61 and 61-62, and the additional hangar can be provided by reducing the OTU CF100 UE in 1960. ADC Sqn UEs will be reduced to 12 aircraft with the introduction of the Arrow; this in turn will reduce the aircrew requirement by 81 crews or a reduction of 25% in AW fighter crews. This should permit a cut-back of at least 10-12 CF100s at the OTU in 60-61 which would provide the extra hangar accommodation required.

      (b)   Therefore, two steel arch hangars could be made available in 1960 for the Arrow evaluation programme by standing down the WPU during the winter of 1960-61 and 61-62 and reducing the 3 (AW) OTU CF100 UE.

Additional Facilities Required

6   **Sparrow Evaluation**

      (a)   TOWED AND DRONE TARGET WORKSHOP. In Jun 58 space will be required for uncrating, assembling and servicing KDA drones.

      (b)   SPARROW LOADING HANGAR. A Guided Missile loading hangar is required by Apr 59.

      (c)   A 4-BAY ALERT HANGAR is being provided to meet the requirements stated in 6(a) and 6(b). Although the Towed and Drone Target Workshop is needed in Jun 58 the 4-bay alert hangar will not be ready before Oct 58.

      (d)   FACILITY FOR SERVICING SPARROW MISSILES. Approval has been sought to modify a portion of the standard armament building already at Cold Lake to meet the requirement for a facility to maintain Sparrow missiles and store support equipment. This accommodation is scheduled to be available by Aug 58.

7   **Arrow Evaluation**

(a)   HANGAR MODIFICATIONS. Electrical power outlets at each aircraft maintenance station to operate main and auxiliary hydraulic rigs, nitrogen compressor, and electronic test equipment. Air conditioning is also required at each aircraft position.

(b)   COVER SPACE FOR GROUND SUPPORT EQUIPMENT. A floor space of at least 8000 ft is needed to service and store mobile ground equipment such as engine starting units, power and cooling air trucks, main hydraulic rigs, nitrogen compressors, engine change equipment and access platforms.

(c)   DATA PROCESSING FACILITY. The existing facility will be enlarged during 58 to meet Sparrow evaluation requirements and further expanded in 1959 to meet Arrow test requirements. It may be possible to house the Data Processing Facility in the cantilever hangar, if not, a new building will be required.

(d)   ASTRA SHOP. This shop will consist of a Fire Control System, an Automatic Flying Control System, Telecommunications and Navigation System facilities. About 10,000 sq ft is required.

(e)   ELECTRICAL SHOP. It is expected that existing facilities will be adequate in respect to floor space.

(f)   INSTRUMENT SHOP. Although additional facilities will be required for servicing and checking new type instruments extra floor space will not be required as the new equipment can be housed in existing shops.

(g)   BATTERY SHOP. An additional battery room will be required to handle the nickel cadmium batteries. About 100 sq ft will be adequate.

(h)   LIQUID OXYGEN CHARGING AND STORAGE. A space about 600 sq ft will be required for charging, servicing and storing Arrow 2 oxygen converters. In addition about 200 sq ft will be needed to accommodate a 500 gal. storage tank and a 50 gal. mobile liquid oxygen trailer.

(j)   ENGINE ACCESSORIES ASSEMBLY AND TEST FACILITY. The accessories assembly shop will require about 2000 sq ft. The engine running facility, which should be located in an area remote from other facilities, will require about 2000 sq ft.

(k)   HYDRAULIC SHOP. This facility requires about 400 sq ft.

(l)   DRAG CHUTES. Space will be required for hanging and storing chutes. Adequate space may be available with existing facilities.

ANNEX 4
To APPENDIX "C"
To Programme of Activities
1958–1962

(m)   TURN-AROUND HANGAR SPACE. A requirement has been registered for two turn-around hangars to effectively demonstrate Arrow state of readiness and "turn-arounds". Two readiness hangars of existing type can be adapted; however, it may be difficult to obtain approval for their construction as there may not be a long term requirement for these hangars at Cold Lake. If this is the case it is recommended that the demonstrations of states of readiness and "turn-arounds" be included in Phase 8 trials where the operational environment is suitable.

Runways

8   On 16 Jan 58; approval was granted for the construction of a 4,300 ft extension to the main runway, complete with the necessary lighting, parking aprons, warm-up pads and taxiways to meet joint needs of the RCAF and USAF. The contract is planned to be let by mid-58 and construction is scheduled for completion by late 59. This will meet Arrow evaluation requirements.

Personnel Accommodation

9   SERVICE PERSONNEL. With 300 PMQs scheduled for completion this year and about 650 single quarters yet to be occupied, no difficulty is foreseen in providing accommodation for service personnel during the Sparrow and Arrow evaluation programme.

10   CONTRACTOR PERSONNEL. Commencing Apr 59, a small number of contractor personnel will be required at Cold Lake to support the Sparrow 2 programme. During the peak Sparrow test period in 59-60 about 60 contractor personnel will be employed in Cold Lake. The requirement for accommodation will increase in Mar 60 when additional personnel arrive for the Arrow tests. To support the four contractor aircraft during the peak period of the contractor conducted trials, the following personnel are required:

Servicing	- 120
Flight Test Engineers	- 80
Miscellaneous	- 10
	210

Of these, 120 must be contractor personnel and about 90 could be RCAF if properly trained. Therefore, during 60-61 accommodation for about 170-180 contractor personnel is required. Beyond 1961 about 60 contractor personnel will be located at Cold Lake to support development to improve Arrow capability.

11   Government approval will be sought to have 100 rental housing units constructed at Grand Centre Alta for contractor personnel assigned to Cold Lake. Subject to obtaining approval and CMHC making the necessary arrangements with a contractor, construction is expected to begin in 1958 with some units available by late 58. This programme should provide sufficient married quarters for contractor personnel.

BASE FOR PHASES 6 AND 8 ARROW TRIALS

1   Phase 6, Intensive Flying, and Phase 8, Operational Suitability Tests, are scheduled to begin in Sep 60 and Feb 61 respectively. Three aircraft have been assigned to Phase 6 and six aircraft to Phase 8. Phases 3, 4, 5 and 7 only of the Arrow evaluation programme can be conducted at Cold Lake because of limited hangar accommodation. Therefore from the hangar availability standpoint alone another base must be selected for Phase 6 and 8.

Factors to Be Considered When Selecting a Base for Phases 6 and 8

2   Although from an evaluation point of view it is not necessary to conduct both phases from the same base shortages in test and maintenance equipment and availability of qualified personnel make it mandatory that Phases 6 and 8 be conducted by the same unit and from the same base.

3   An ADC base should be selected because:

(a)   Modifications to base facilities supporting the programme can be readily adapted to sqn operations on completion of the trials; and

(b)   A better evaluation of logistic support and base facility requirements can be obtained if the trials were conducted from an established ADC base

4   Phase 8 must be conducted within the SAGE environment as one of the key factors in the operational suitability trials is the programming of the aircraft into a SAGE computer. Phase 8 trials are scheduled for Feb – Jul 61 and even if a Canadian SAGE sector is approved installation would not be completed by this date. Therefore there are only two alternatives:

(a)   Carry out the trials from an ADC base which is covered by an American SAGE sector, or

(b)   Seek permission to use a USAF base within the SAGE environment.

Uplands as a Possible Site for Phases 6 and 8

5   HANGARS.   Hangar accommodation can be provided at Uplands by allotting one of the steel arch hangars completed this year to the OPU. From Feb to Apr 61 Phases 6 and 8 overlap 9 Arrow aircraft require accommodation during this peak period. One Sqn or CEPE may have to give up space in a steel arch hangar until Phase 6 is completed. Hangar modifications will be required to provide power and air conditioning outlets.

6   RUNWAYS. 8800 ft available with no overshoots. 10,000 square feet has been stated as the requirement for Arrow testing. Barriers will be needed if the runway is not extended.

ANNEX 5
To APPENDIX "C"
To Programme of Activities
1958–1962

---

7   PERSONNEL ACCOMMODATION. About 400 personnel will be involved in supporting Phase 6 and 8. Approximately 75% of this total will come from units other than Uplands. Therefore additional accommodation may be required.

8   ALERT HANGARS. Two readiness hangars of the existing type are required to evaluate states of readiness and "turn-around" capability of the aircraft.

9   SYNTHETIC TRAINERS. Space to accommodate as Aircraft Systems Trainer and an Operational Flight and Tactics Trainer is required.

10   ADDITIONAL FACILITIES. Space for ground support equipment, a complete Astra shop; a Liquid Oxygen charging and storage facility; Hydraulic Shop; engine shop with silenced run-up facility and missile maintenance and storage accommodation is required.